Praise for *Sustaining*

T0276345

"Aptly titled, this book provides a realistic perspe.... ...
lenges of, to use a metaphor, changing the tires on your car while
you are driving on the freeway. Powe and Weems provide a handy,
thoughtful, practical, and inspirational book focused on leading
churches through today's disruptive environment, rather than play-
ing it safe by continuing a steady decline into obsolescence. The
wisdom they provide extends to any for-purpose organization."
— Barry Z. Posner, Accolti Endowed Professor
of Leadership; chair, department of management
and entrepreneurship, Leavey School of Business,
Santa Clara University; and coauthor of
The Leadership Challenge and *Everyday
People, Extraordinary Leadership*

"*Sustaining While Disrupting* achieves the rare feat of being
timely and timeless. The practical tips will be a welcomed by
those who love the church but see it struggling to be fruitful today.
At the same time, the insights on these pages have the potential
to reverberate for generations of church leaders to come. Powe
and Weems have offered us a precious gift. May we sit in the ten-
sions of its truth and be compelled toward vibrancy at the nexus
point of sustaining while disrupting!"
— Heber Brown III, executive director,
The Black Church Food Security Network

"If I could choose one book to give congregational presidents
and pastors this year, it would be the one you hold in your hands.
Nothing is more important (and more challenging) than leading communities in the practices of sustaining and innovating,
both essential to Christian faithfulness. In these readable pages,
Powe and Weems provide the biblical grounding, contextual
urgency, and practical wisdom for sustaining beloved communities while also disrupting them with faithful innovation."
— Ann Svennungsen, bishop, Minneapolis Area Synod,
Evangelical Lutheran Church in America

"*Sustaining While Disrupting* is precisely the correct title for this outstanding book. Church leaders know we live in an era of convergence and divergence. This moment is not new for the church. But many books about congregations lean on demographics or business models. Maintaining while innovating is soul work in all realms of life, however, including congregational life. Refreshingly, Powe and Weems use theological reflection as the foundation for a transformative design, shaping their propositions based on the struggles of the council in Jerusalem as represented in Acts. They also offer tools and skills as gifts for the long haul, not a quick fix. Read, discern, act, and celebrate the wide-open future of the church."

—Tim Shapiro, president,
Center for Congregations

"I found myself taking notes in every chapter as I read *Sustaining While Disrupting*. In a disorienting, pandemic-impacted time, Weems and Powe offer in this timely book clear insights, practical strategies, and abundant wisdom for church leaders on how to take faithful next steps in ministry and leadership."

—Tom Berlin, lead pastor,
Floris United Methodist Church, and author of
Courage: Jesus and the Call to Brave Faith

SUSTAINING WHILE DISRUPTING

SUSTAINING
WHILE
DISRUPTING

THE CHALLENGE OF
CONGREGATIONAL
INNOVATION

F. Douglas Powe Jr.
Lovett H. Weems Jr.

Fortress Press
Minneapolis

SUSTAINING WHILE DISRUPTING
The Challenge of Congregational Innovation

Cover design: L. Owens

Print ISBN: 978-1-5064-7920-0
eBook ISBN: 978-1-5064-7921-7

To the farsighted builders who established the Lewis Center for Church Leadership; to the staff, advisors, and donors who sustain it; and to two visionary seminary presidents, G. Douglass Lewis and David McAllister-Wilson

Contents

Introduction

Many congregations with long histories and proud traditions find themselves facing challenges beyond what they have faced in the lifetimes of their members and pastors. Such challenges are most noticeable in those denominations often referred to as *mainline*, but other churches may recognize that they are facing similar challenges.

After dominating the US religious landscape for much of the country's history, most mainline churches began declining in size and influence after the mid-1960s. Within the next few years, all the mainline denominations would move from membership growth to decline. The consequences of the massive membership losses spanning over fifty years were mitigated by increased giving. It was not unusual for contributions and assets to increase even as membership and attendance declined. However, the even sharper declines in the first decades of the twenty-first century are receiving the attention of church leaders as downward trends become less sustainable. Money can be a lagging and deceptive indicator for churches, as finances can stay strong well after other indicators turn down. Today, however, income increases can no longer be assumed. Many churches have yet to rebound from the financial recession in the first decade of the new century.

Past success does not guarantee future success. It is hard for well-established organizations to adjust to changing

1

circumstances. Size and age can serve churches well, but as contexts change, these same factors make it difficult for them to adjust to new situations. Nimbleness and heritage do not always appear together. Momentum from past success is likely to make it more difficult for official church leaders to recognize major societal changes. The cherished forms of ministry no longer connect with people in the same way as a half century ago. These practices no longer carry the "new wine" of new times. Leaders are pressed to preserve the old forms, only making it harder for them, together with their congregations, to discern the "new thing" God is doing.

UNDERSTANDINGS OF LEADERSHIP

From its beginning, the church has recognized the need for persons to be set apart for leadership within the community. Leadership is essential for religious communities because it is what links past and future. Religious leaders at the same time teach and preserve past traditions and lead the faithful into a future in which those traditions take new shapes to fit new contexts. In this sense, they bridge past and future. Pastoral leadership is set within the context of the ministry that all Christians have through their baptism. Therefore, pastoral leadership is never solely about the personal authority and actions of the clergy but rather about the unfolding drama of the people of God seeking a faithful future for their traditions and communities. Pastoral leaders are central to church leadership but only to the extent that they engage seriously in their tradition, constituents, and context. Pastoral leadership is a response to God's love and action in the world, revealed most clearly in Jesus Christ. Christian leadership is about the fulfillment of that vision.[1]

Understandings of leadership that have shaped *pastoral* leadership come not only from biblical and theological sources but from larger cultural views of leadership as they have evolved over time. For religious leadership, Max Weber's distinction in 1922 between "priest" and "prophet" has been useful.[2] The priest leads within an established group with norms and standards. The prophet is an agent of change who challenges the established order. Pastoral leaders lead from the center of religious institutions (priest) and from the edge of established patterns (prophet). To some leaders, such deference to the theological and liturgical values of long traditions will seem excessive. To others, such care for heritage will hinder their passion to travel new and unfamiliar roads in search of God's preferred future.

Pastoral leaders are constantly navigating between the attempt to sustain the tradition and, at the same time, the urge to move in a new direction to achieve more fully the missions of their congregations. At one time, leaders were confident this was possible because they knew the problem and had a solution. If the youth ministry was lagging, the solution was to hire a youth director. The problems faced today by mainline leadership are often what Ronald Heifetz calls "adaptive challenges," in which the problem is uncertain, the solution is uncertain, or both are uncertain.[3] A generational disconnect between youth and church cannot be solved by hiring staff. As with any adaptive challenge, a season of learning is essential to address such situations.[4] Those writing today about pastoral leadership often use language of paradox and ambiguity to capture how difficult the leadership challenge now is. Although church historian E. Brooks Holifield reminds his readers that clergy in the United States have commonly had to lead within such paradox and ambiguity,[5] it is in such a challenging environment that mainline pastoral leaders are today asked to serve.

CHALLENGES FACING PASTORAL LEADERS TODAY

Many pastoral leaders today are serving churches whose congregations believe their best years were in the past. What a shame. In so many ways, the fields are ready for harvest today, and there are a great number of indicators that churches should be at the forefront of contemporary challenges. The growing diversity of the United States and the concurrent rise in racial intolerance come as most religious traditions affirm inclusiveness and mutual respect. Yet the culture has changed to such an extent that there is a misalignment between the typical church of today and the communities of today. People often forget that their memories of past church vitality came when their church's connection with the community was much stronger. Church memberships, to a large extent, no longer reflect the community around them. Church constituencies today are often older, less diverse, more educated, more affluent, and more likely to be married than their communities. Without strong community connections or the social pressures and norms of Christendom, churches find it hard to thrive in an "open market" where they must make their place alongside myriad other entities vying for the attention and loyalty of a skeptical public. Yet the opportunities remain vast.

REACHING MORE PEOPLE

Perhaps the greatest contrast of many churches within their contexts is the consistent decline in their constituencies amid population growth. The failure to reach the people of their communities, especially those different from their current constituents, hampers the church's mission. Decline is accepted as normal by some pastoral leaders who have never served during a time of growth in the denominations. Pastoral leaders with neither a passion for reaching new people nor an expectation that it is possible to do so have little chance of guiding congregations to expand their reach within their communities. Indeed, churches in the United States have a viable future only to the extent that they can develop capacities for calling, passion, and plans essential to reach more people, more diverse people, and younger people.

REACHING MORE DIVERSE PEOPLE

Churches in the United States have a history of attracting similar people. Many traditions that began with a mixture of races soon succumbed to the social constraints of race. For example, when Bishop Francis Asbury, the guiding leader of American Methodism, died in 1816, about one-quarter of Methodists were African American. Such diversity did not last. At the same time, many people of color in mixed-race churches were finding that their place was not one of equality, thus making the formation of churches especially for them more attractive. The larger narrative of racial separation and segregation came to dominate church life as it did public life.

Just a few decades ago, most congregations served a single race. There are fewer and fewer churches each year made up of one race only. However, the movement to multiracial churches where no one racial group makes up 80 percent or more of the constituents has been much slower in coming.

Even beyond race, churches have also tended to serve distinctive cohorts within the population based on other factors such as income and education. This approach is somewhat a result of where churches are located, but often a greater barrier to a richer diversity comes from an array of practices and assumptions such as music, worship, preaching, and dress that make a church less inviting to some than to others.

Many churches continue to struggle to include persons from a broad social and economic range. The need for a church inclusive of all people is paramount today, given the church's stated values, the teachings of the gospel, and the diversity of the United States. A church known for exclusiveness has little future among the young, who not only are far more diverse than any other age sector of the population but also assume diversity and notice when it is absent. The growing racial and ethnic diversity of the United States will shape the future of all institutions in ways hard to imagine. A church's appeal to new constituents will be shaped largely by its ability to respond to the changing face of the nation.

REACHING YOUNGER PEOPLE

Countless churches are aging churches. The aging membership of many congregations has been a continuing concern for many years, and for good reason. For a large segment of churches, certainly including all the mainline traditions, it seems clear that since at least the 1970s, the trend has been toward serving a membership older than the general population. The death rate of church members compared to that of the general population is one indicator of an aging church. Churches that as late as the mid-1960s may have had death rates lower than those of the general population now consistently surpass national death rates considerably. Another factor contributing to the aging phenomenon is that birth rates among the traditional constituencies of many denominations are lower than those of the nation. The goal of reaching younger people is about not survival but faithfulness to the church's mission. Teaching the faith to new generations has motivated churches throughout time. Continuity of a faith's beliefs, values, and outreach is at stake.

SERVING THE COMMON GOOD

Yesterday's church has no power to attract newer generations. The inward orientation of so many churches is a barrier to those who share little loyalty to tradition but passionately care about making a difference in the lives of people and their communities. Churches that pursue their own welfare apart from a commitment to the common good of their communities will have little to offer the young and others not already connected with churches.

While no *one* thing is the absolute key to reengaging with people not currently reached by the church, one practice that could go a long way toward this goal is for churches to show love and concern for their communities, as they did in the early days of their histories. The longer a church has been in existence, the less knowledgeable it is likely to be about its community and the less connected it becomes with that community. Although that sounds strange, it is rare that a long-existing church is more aware of the trends, demographics, and movements of its community than a new congregation in that same place. In a community, one of the churches was founded 150 years ago. Another church began having worship services six months ago. Of these two, which will have their fingers on the pulse of the community the best? Even if one has a head start of 150 years, it's the newer congregation that will know more about what is happening now.

In its early years, a congregation gives careful attention to the community, its people, and their needs. Otherwise, the church does not take root and survive. When a congregation achieves the critical mass needed to sustain a new church, the focus begins to change. Many congregations then become worlds unto themselves, lacking active engagement with their surroundings and the ways they are changing. Without a careful plan to stay close to the heartbeat of one's surroundings, internal considerations dominate. Then, when growth turns to decline, it is even harder for churches to reverse their internal preoccupations. Many of the practices that led to initial growth are no longer in place or have not adapted to new situations. The factors that lead to a decline in existing constituents also make it less likely that new people will join. Whether congregations are facing a loss of energy in worship, music, outreach, or age ministries, there are fewer exciting entry points needed for growth.[6]

THIS BOOK

This book gives church leaders in established congregations theological insights and practical skills for two crucial tasks: to sustain and strengthen foundational elements of their churches and to guide the critical innovation required to serve a context vastly different from the one in which many current assumptions and behaviors were established as normative.

How do you sustain and innovate at the same time? The truth is that most mainline denominations, and even non-denominational congregations, are set up to sustain what is already in place. Of course, this makes practical sense. Most congregations are not new church starts but have been in existence for a long enough period that leaders are seeking to keep what is in place going. The reality is that theological education and denominational training focus on sustaining what already exists.

Thinking about innovation often takes a back seat to the daily tasks of leadership. It is not that leaders are necessarily opposed to trying something new. One of the main challenges is learning to take risks in a system that rewards perpetuating what already exists. For instance, if I am the pastor of a congregation that averages eighty to ninety people in worship and my parishioners like the way things are going, it is unlikely that I will try something new even if no one new has joined us for worship in the last five years. The prospect of trying something that could bring in new individuals seems too risky compared to maintaining the status quo.

The dilemma of sustaining while innovating is challenging for leaders. This book will help them navigate this dilemma. We will offer insights for reinterpreting the priest and prophet paradigm in a manner that does not make them oppositional. We will help leaders stay connected to those currently supporting the congregation while also helping them reach more people. Being a leader today is not an either/or proposition but requires a commitment to sustaining and innovating.

Chapter 1

Sustaining and Innovating
A BIBLICAL MODEL

The challenge with using a particular lens and applying it to the Bible is that you can easily create a paradigm to fit what you are seeking. It is our hope to avoid this trap but at the same time illustrate that the church was birthed in a manner that was both sustaining and innovating. It is in the book of Acts that we find the birth narrative of the church. This narrative includes stories about sustaining the key ideals of the church and expanding its configuration (the Way) to include the gentiles.

ACTS 15

Acts 15 illustrates the tension between sustaining and innovating. One place this tension is played out is in the dispute over the need for gentiles to be circumcised (vv. 1–2). Those seeking to maintain the Jewish tradition argue for alignment with the law of Moses and claim that circumcision is necessary. Paul and Barnabas argue for thinking about circumcision as not simply physical and for expanding what this tradition means so it can be more inclusive. So a council is called in Jerusalem to settle the dispute.

If you read from Acts 1 to 15, it does not take long to figure out that the explicit dispute focusing on circumcision is really camouflaging a core issue: "How do we faithfully pursue God's calling?" The question is one way of framing the central issue the church faces not only in Acts 15 but throughout the first part of the book. We continue to ask this question today, but we often answer it differently depending on whether we focus on sustaining or innovating.

In Acts 15:5, the Pharisees are seeking to faithfully pursue God's calling by upholding the law of Moses. Distinguished Baylor University New Testament scholar Beverly Gaventa refers to the Pharisees as "Christian Pharisees" who are concerned that certain theological traditions are upheld.[1] They are committed to Jesus's message but believe the way to pursue it is to maintain certain ideals. Paul and Barnabas are seeking to faithfully pursue God's calling by expanding the way one understands circumcision. Of course, Paul and Barnabas also are committed to Jesus's message, but they emphasize that God is doing a new thing with the gentiles.[2] Peter gives credence to this expanded understanding when he shares with the council that the Holy Spirit fell on the gentiles as well as the Jews (Acts 15:8). God did not discriminate based on physical circumcision. While both groups are ultimately seeking to pursue God's calling, the struggle is to do so in a manner that sustains and innovates at the same time. Before we get to the both/and solution the council offers, let us explore how the church in Acts sustains and innovates.

SUSTAINING

In Acts 1:8, we see a passing of the torch of sorts from Jesus to the apostles. Jesus states, "You will receive power when the Holy Spirit comes on you; and you will be my witnesses in Jerusalem, and in all Judea and Samaria, and to the ends of the earth" (1:8 NIV). The apostles will be empowered to continue the work Jesus started locally by sharing the gospel to the ends of the earth. Throughout the early chapters of Acts, the apostles do this by teaching and performing miracles in the region.[3] As the heirs of the Holy Spirit, they strengthen the community started by Jesus. The Holy Spirit empowers them to sustain the work Jesus started.

In Acts 2, on the day of Pentecost, all are filled with the Spirit. The Spirit allows those gathered who are Jewish or converts to Judaism to hear one another speaking in their native tongue. Peter, one of the apostles, confirms this miracle by addressing the crowd as "fellow Jews and all of you who live in Jerusalem" (Acts 2:14). Peter is clear that the movement Jesus started is for the Jewish community and that they must continue to nurture it going forward. At this point, what we now call Christianity is rooted in Judaism. The work that Peter and the other apostles are doing to nurture the movement culminates in Acts 2:42–47, where the apostles are established as the leaders of the community, which is growing in numbers. A shift occurs whereby Jesus moves from leading the community to becoming its central message. The apostles believe their role is to sustain Jesus's message, teaching, and works within the Jewish community.

Let us share three observations about the apostles' sustaining work from this part of the biblical text. First, sustainers believe they are continuing a tradition and not creating their own. Second, sustainers interpret the tradition from the perspective of insiders, not outsiders. Third, sustainers are interested in practices that embody Jesus's message and life with the disciples. They do all this to faithfully pursue God's calling.

CONTINUING A TRADITION

When Peter addresses the crowd in Acts 2, he begins by quoting the prophet Joel to ground his remarks within the Jewish tradition. Peter does alter Joel's words to connect to the outpouring of the Spirit.[4] But he maintains the central message that God is continuing the work of prophecy, thus linking the current community to Joel's and establishing that the work of this new community is a continuation of the work that God has always done. The new faith community that is taking shape is not a breakaway from the tradition; it is a continuation of the tradition.

When we consider framing our work in congregations as a continuation of the early church, we can think about it in two ways. First, we see ourselves linked to and carrying on the traditions started by the first Christians. This is why we celebrate communion and participate in baptism. Certainly, denominations may practice communion and baptism differently, but the connection to the tradition is almost universal.

We also must be mindful of our particular congregational traditions that get passed down for generations. For instance, a congregation may have a tradition of singing only denominational hymns on second Sundays. This tradition is unique to a particular congregation but may date back decades. Sustaining this practice is one way of connecting the generations within the congregation and keeping the congregation connected to the denomination.

The point is that we are sustaining not only Christian traditions but also congregational traditions. For many of us who are part of a denomination, those traditions also must be considered. For instance, the Evangelical Lutheran Church in America (ELCA) refers to its governing body as a *synod*, while Methodists use the term *conference*. In both instances, the choice of language has roots in tradition related to the origin of the denomination. Peter and the first Christian community believed sustaining tradition to be important, and we continue to follow in their footsteps by doing the same thing today. In part, this is how we faithfully live out God's calling—by continuing traditions that have shaped and, we believe, will continue to shape the community.

INTERPRETING

In Acts 2, Peter begins interpreting the importance of Jesus in light of the tradition. In verse 30, he claims that God promised David, a prophet, that a descendant of his would be placed upon his throne. Jesus is the Messiah who fulfills this promise. Of course, Peter is building on the connection between David and Jesus that the writer of Luke–Acts establishes in the genealogy narrative (Luke 3:23–28). He interprets the meaning of Jesus's ministry from the perspective of one inside the tradition. Jesus's purpose is to fulfill that which has already been prophesied, not to create something new. In this manner, Peter's interpretation sustains the ongoing tradition and narrative of both Jesus's message and the Jewish tradition.

Congregations often sustain tradition by interpreting the multifaceted congregational narrative discussed earlier through the lens of their faith community. Consider an Episcopal African American congregation seeking racial equity within the denomination. Leaders and members likely see this work as sustaining the message that we are all the same within the body of Christ (highlighted in Gal 3:28). They also worship in a manner that any Episcopal congregation, whether white or African American, would recognize. Interpreting their faith in this way is consistent with being Episcopalian and the challenges of being African American. They do not perceive themselves as doing something new but believe they are being consistent with the biblical narrative. Or consider a white evangelical church that promotes family values as central to the gospel message (in light of 1 Tim 3:2–5). Similar to the African American congregation, the evangelical congregation does not see itself as doing something new; they see their work as part of the Christian narrative that promotes the values in which their faith is grounded.

In both cases, the interpretation (whether we agree or disagree with it) is an insider perspective about what is important in that community as it relates to the multifaceted Christian narrative. Peter interprets Jesus's ministry in light of Jesus's claim, as the rightful heir, to the throne of David. For those in the first-century Christian Jewish community, this understanding of Jesus shapes their worldview. The African American and evangelical congregations are making interpretive moves similar to those of the first-century Christian Jewish community to fit their worldviews. Our point is not that an interpretation is right or wrong. Our point is that an insider perspective influences the way we see the narrative.

If a congregation is seeking to start a children's ministry, it is not unusual for it to look at the age of its current children and build the ministry around them. This makes sense because the goal is to keep those who are supporting the congregation happy. Starting a youth ministry for teens when all the children are between the ages of six and eight probably would not go over well with some in the congregation. The insider view influences how many in the congregation are interpreting the Christian narrative at that point. They are concerned with their needs, and this becomes the worldview out of which the Christian narrative is interpreted.

PRACTICES

In Acts 2:42, we read that the community is engaging in learning, sharing resources, and eating together. Following Peter's speech about Jesus, we learn how the Acts 2:42–47 community puts into practice what the apostles learned as a means of continuing the tradition and interpreting the narrative. We believe one way of thinking about these practices is that the community is continuing to embody what was handed down from Jesus. By doing these things, the apostles are reenacting their time with Jesus.

In the same manner, congregations today align tradition, interpretation, and practice. We are not suggesting this alignment is done on purpose (often it is not), but it often happens by virtue of the way sustaining the congregational identity and work almost becomes second nature. Congregations make decisions based on what is prudent given their history, circumstances, finances, and so forth. If we stick with the Episcopal African American congregation and imagine a history of civil rights engagement based on an interpretation of the text as viewed through the lens of equality, then it is no surprise that the congregation shapes even a practice like worship around justice-oriented themes. The congregation may not realize that this is what it is doing, however, because embodying justice-related themes has become second nature.

We have highlighted in the Acts 2 text the importance of continuing traditions, interpreting a multifaceted Christian narrative, and faithfully embodying Jesus's message to the disciples. All three actions illustrate how the early church sustained ministry. These are not the only ways in which today's congregations are sustaining, but these three themes emerging from Acts are still relevant today. The ways in which we draw from these themes are at times invisible to us because our focus is on keeping things moving in the congregation. This can lead to wanting to keep the status quo because it is familiar and fits our current worldview. When you think of these themes, it is easy to see why a contingent in Acts 15 would argue that circumcision is necessary. They see it through the lens of sustaining what is already happening. By continuing circumcision, they are faithfully following God's calling. But this is just a part of the story in the first half of Acts, so we now turn to innovating.

INNOVATING

In Acts 10, we read another story involving Peter, but this one is about innovation. Although Peter is a primary character, the story actually begins with Cornelius, a centurion in the Italian regiment. Cornelius has a vision, and later in chapter 10, Peter also has a vision. Both men find their visions to be unorthodox, and the visions, which involve gentiles and Jews associating with one another, catch them by surprise. In Cornelius's vision, the God of Israel asks him, a gentile, to send for Peter, a Jew. Peter's vision is about eating food prohibited by law because it is unclean. We can imagine the visions are troubling to both because they do not fit with their worldviews and if shared with others in their community probably would cause those individuals to question the sanity of Peter and Cornelius.

Following these visions, we read about an innovation regarding who is a part of the community. The visions open up the possibilities of sharing the message given to the disciples with the gentiles. The expansion of the church's mission to the gentiles gives us three clues about the importance of innovation. First, innovation starts outside the community and not within it. Second, innovation requires a willingness to take risks. Third, innovation requires putting aside previously held convictions. As we unpack these themes, it becomes obvious that engaging in innovation also leads to faithfully following God's calling.

THINKING LIKE AN OUTSIDER

These visions are framed by Acts 9, where we read about the conversion of Saul, a diaspora Jew from Asia Minor. Saul, later named Paul, persecuted the Jews before his conversion and is an outsider among the apostles who walked with Jesus. In verse 15, the Lord reports to Ananias that Saul will carry his message to the gentiles and secondarily to the people of Israel. That is, an outsider (though one who is still Jewish) is going to take the message to outsiders.

In chapter 10, God first speaks to Cornelius, who is a gentile, and not to Peter, who is one of the apostles. God tells Cornelius to send men to bring Peter back to Cornelius's house. Certainly, it was out of the ordinary that a gentile would send for someone of the Jewish faith to come to his house, but Cornelius does as he is instructed. A day later, Peter has a vision about killing and eating what observant Jews considered unclean food. At first Peter resists, but after receiving the vision three times, he starts to ponder the meaning of this extraordinary message. The message Peter is receiving will mean no longer sustaining an insider's understanding of God working only through the Jewish community but promoting innovation by reaching out to a community that is outside of the Jewish tradition. For Peter, the sign that such an innovation is really from God is that Cornelius's men find him.

It is highly unlikely that Peter would have considered going with Cornelius's men if it were not for his own vision. It is also highly unlikely that Peter would have on his own decided to take the gospel message to the gentiles. Peter required some impetus from the outside to get him to start thinking differently about the possibilities for God's salvific message. Peter is an insider, and although he is creative, his perspective is focused on embodying the narrative in a particular way. Not until he is presented with another perspective is he able to see new possibilities.

Like Peter, many of us who are leaders in the church embody the narrative in a certain way. We may be creative, but we are creative at sustaining. Unfortunately, we do not always listen for the voice of God spoken through outsiders who can help us see new possibilities. Think about this scenario: a congregation wants to start a new worship service so it can reach more diverse people. It begins by pulling together church leaders to figure out what is possible. They come up with a plan and some new music offerings that feature a guitar instead of an organ. The congregation is surprised and disappointed when no one shows up except for a few members of the church.

Still hoping to reach a more diverse body, this time the congregation begins by doing focus groups with those in the community and connecting them to their social media offerings. They learn that offering a contemplative experience for stay-at-home parents would be a gift to the community. They work with a few focus group participants to create such an experience and are delighted that a core group participates weekly. The difference is that the first effort sustained what they already did because it was still a reflection of those on the inside. In the second scenario, they enlisted input from outsiders and were able to innovate (contemplative services are not new, but they are new for them).

It is possible to innovate as an insider, but it is more challenging. The innovation of taking the message to the gentiles does not come from those inside the community. It comes from outside of the community. In the same manner, congregations that seek the input of outsiders are often more innovative because the outsiders, with different perspectives, see new possibilities.

TAKING RISKS

Innovation always entails risk. In the Acts text, Cornelius takes a risk by calling Peter, a Jew, to come to his home. Peter takes a risk by going to meet Cornelius, a gentile centurion. Peter names this risk in 10:28 when he addresses the gathered crowd: "It is against our law for a Jew to associate with or visit a gentile. But God has shown me that I should not call anyone impure or unclean" (NIV). God has given him a new vision. There is risk for both Peter and Cornelius (Jews and gentiles) to live into the vision that God has put before them. It is Cornelius's and Peter's willingness to take risks that opens the door for greater possibilities.

The decision to move forward can be challenging and contentious. Even Peter had to see his vision three times before it really took hold, before he was willing to break the law against associating with gentiles. Congregations today may find themselves in a situation where taking risks is necessary for opening the door to greater possibilities. In many instances, a risk requires going against an embedded tradition or practice. In congregations, considering this type of risk-taking may play out in terms of theological traditions or something as practical as doing away with printed copies of the bulletin.

Continuing this example, doing away with printed copies of the bulletin becomes contentious when individuals who feel like they are losing more than they are gaining start pushing back. The loss of what is familiar overshadows the possibility of what may be new and exciting, like other ways of communicating the liturgy for in-person and virtual audiences. These individuals make comments like "We have always had printed bulletins." The danger is that when things become contentious, the purpose of the innovation gets lost in all the bickering. Yes, taking a risk can have unforeseen or unpleasant consequences. As we will discuss later, the key is developing a plan for these upfront. But at this point, we want to emphasize that innovating requires taking risks that often move individuals out of their comfort zones and, at the same time, open them up to seeing new possibilities.

Taking a risk just for the sake of it is not helpful; a risk must be calculated. Cornelius and Peter take what they perceive to be calculated risks based on the visions both receive. A calculated risk moves us toward something new that still is embedded in what we are called to live out. It is not done simply to shock others. Peter and Cornelius are taking a calculated risk because what they are doing is still embedded in the belief that God can act in the lives of the gentiles. Their goal is not simply to get attention by saying, "Look what we are doing in taking the Jewish Christian faith to those outside of the law!" We have to be careful that we are genuinely trying to live into God's calling in a new way.

PUTTING ASIDE CONVICTIONS

One of the most challenging risks for anyone to take is to put aside previously held convictions. When we believe something to be true and have lived like it is true, to pivot and see things differently is challenging. For instance, it was a challenge for many congregations (and still is for some) to accept women pastors. This went against previously held convictions. But for the pioneer congregations who accepted women pastors, it was a risk because they were going against the cultural grain. Cornelius and his family are described as God-fearing people. Scholars debate what this really means. One possibility is that he worshipped Israel's God as an uncircumcised individual and had not completed the process of conversion to Judaism.[5] For our purposes, it is fair to assume that Cornelius never imagined being accepted into the newly formed Jewish Christian faith community because he was an outsider, not a Jew.

Peter has this same conviction coming from another perspective. He never pictured a world in which Jews and gentiles would openly associate with one another in a faith community. Following Jewish tradition, he was convinced that the gentiles were "unclean." The visions Cornelius and Peter each receive disrupt these convictions. They point to a different possibility that is foreign to both.

Putting aside convictions for congregations today is never easy. We are talking about not just theological convictions, which are especially difficult to set aside, but convictions regarding who should get use of the church facility or what instruments should be allowed in worship. When we are convinced that something is right, it can be challenging to alter our perspectives even when it is necessary. Individuals in a congregation convinced that they can worship only on Sunday probably will have a hard time considering worshipping on a Thursday.

Often something from the outside (returning to our first point) must prick the imaginations of those holding on to their set ways to see that something else is possible. For Peter and Cornelius, that something was visions from God. While we are still receiving visions from God today, something as simple as the offhand comment of a visitor might be what pricks our imagination. The point is that innovating requires dealing with long-held convictions, especially those that are near and dear to us. Until we confront them, we are not likely to do something innovative.

WHAT IS YOUR ROLE?

We need to distinguish between promoting innovation and carrying it out. Peter is God's instrument to begin the innovation, but it is Paul and Barnabas who make it a reality. Acts 11:20 reports that the good news is spread to Greeks in Antioch. In chapter 13, we learn that Barnabas and Paul are enlisted to spread the word even farther, to Cyprus, and a gentile faith community is formed under their guidance.

Our role may be to promote the innovation in a manner similar to Peter's. Our role may be to carry it out, as Barnabas and Paul did. In either case, it is important to discern our role and to be comfortable with the fact that someone else has a different role. Peter is instrumental in expanding the good news to the gentiles, but his work is with the established Jerusalem faith community. For the innovation to take hold, Barnabas and Paul need to travel to a new place, to take an even bigger risk.

One way of approaching innovation is to pay attention to outsiders who can help us see the world through different lenses, creating an alternative worldview. We get a small hint of this with Peter and Cornelius even though God is the main agent acting to bring them together. When they share what God has revealed with each other, it allows them to see the world from the view of an outsider—doing so while seeking to faithfully follow God's calling.

SUSTAINING AND INNOVATING

Returning to the Acts 15 text with which we began this chapter, we now have a clearer picture of the ways in which some early church leaders were sustainers and others were innovators. Both groups sought to faithfully follow God's calling. The council at Jerusalem demonstrates that ultimately, faithfulness requires both sustaining and innovating.

Before the council reaches this decision, a robust discussion takes place (v. 7). It is when Peter, an insider of the faith, shares his story that those in the council engage the work of Paul and Barnabas differently. Peter speaks as one who is invested in sustaining what Jesus started. We should not underestimate today the importance of an insider supporting an innovative effort. Other insiders trust this individual and will give greater credence to what they say than someone from the outside. It is only after Peter speaks that Paul and Barnabas offer testimony about the work they are doing. The audience is more open to hearing and digesting their words because of Peter's support.

In verse 19, the council decides to lessen the burden on gentiles who want to join the community. The decision honors both the sustaining and the innovating taking place. It is important to note that even though innovation is accepted, the group expects that some laws will need to be observed (v. 20). The real gift is that the gentiles will not have to practice circumcision to become a part of the community. The council finds a way to sustain what Jesus started by upholding the Jewish tradition and to expand on it by including gentiles in a way that innovates on the tradition.

There will likely always be a tension between faithfully following God as a sustainer or as an innovator. We can do both in a manner that upholds the core of Jesus's message. We can learn from the council that faithfully following God's calling is not a matter of either sustaining or innovating. It is often a both/and proposition that requires a community of faith to open itself to new possibilities, such as the possibility that the person or group leading the sustaining effort does not also lead the innovating effort or that the one who promotes innovating does not also make it happen.

The book of Acts helps us see that for the church to faithfully follow God's calling, it must continually sustain and innovate. The truth is that neither one of these is easy to do today. It is easy to sustain the wrong things and lose sight of what God is calling us toward. We can fall into the trap of innovating to be a part of the next fad. We will always face challenges in the work of sustaining and innovating. But when we faithfully seek to follow God's calling, the work of sustaining and innovating can help us see possibilities we never imagined, possibilities like the experience of Peter, Cornelius, and Paul.

Chapter 2

The Pastoral Leadership Dilemma

Starting a new church, with all its challenges and uncertainties, requires a special kind of leadership. Equally challenging is the experience of many more pastors who serve well-established congregations with budgets, buildings, and people. The challenges presented by the uncertainty of the new church start are replaced in established churches with expectations about what the future should be, though it is generally assumed to be a continuation of the present. Each of the existing structures, practices, values, and customs brings with it an embedded culture that provides strength for continuity as well as resistance to change.

Some established churches are thriving and growing, but they are exceptions. The longer a church has been in existence, the less likely it is to show attendance growth. Many of the reasons for this reality are the same as those that make leading in such situations challenging and require a special kind of creativity. For established churches that are thriving, the common denominator is that they have found ways to change to meet new situations. Leaders of these churches recognize that the current state of things is never synonymous with God's ultimate will. Unfortunately, the unspoken mission of many churches is the theologically unjustifiable hope to "stay as good as we are."

Churches may resist change even more than other organizations, and often for good reason. The church is shaped by tradition and heritage—beliefs, customs, rituals, and shared assumptions. Other established organizations are bound together by such elements, but the church wraps its customs with a divine blessing that few other groups claim. Still, churches do change, as is obvious from comparing church life today with that of a century or even a generation ago. However, the church does not change quickly. Today's changing cultural attitudes often require a nimbleness unknown among most churches. Churches might recognize how ill-equipped they are to serve in this new world yet feel helpless to do anything different.

Indeed, change is inherent in our theological heritage. We are always pilgrims seeking the promised land of God's greatest hopes and desires for us. The people of God have always been on a journey requiring repentance, forgiveness, renewal, and trust. The word *new* is not strange to the Christian vocabulary. People of faith are always seeking the new humanity, new creation, and New Jerusalem that God has for us. We easily confuse the earthen vessels with the real treasure God has for us, however. The gospel calls us to put our trust not in our own ingenuity but in God, who we believe "is able to accomplish abundantly far more than all we can ask or imagine" (Eph 3:20).

Successful and lasting change comes more through evolution than revolution, however. That is, genuine change involves continuity. Most congregations operate out of histories that will shape their futures even when they move in new directions. Even so, evolutionary leadership can produce revolutionary results, although it appears revolutionary only in retrospect. People look back and say, "We could never have dreamed this when we first started."[1]

As we have seen, leadership requires change as a theological imperative, and change requires leaders. In the church, these leaders are shaped more by the basics of their faith and the context in which they serve than by their personalities or comfort zones. Leaders will need to express this special kind of leadership in ways that are consistent with who they are, but the leader's goal is not so much "to be me" but to do God's will with the people God has given them.

THE LEADER AS SUSTAINER AND INNOVATOR

Innovation and ongoing operations are always and inevitably in conflict.

—Vijay Govindarajan and Chris Trimble,
The Other Side of Innovation

Doing God's will as the leader of your congregation will be shaped by the context in which you are serving and the season of the church's life in which you and God's people find yourselves. You do not always have a choice as to whether you will primarily be a sustainer or an innovator, and the reality is that you will be challenged to be both.

Few leaders manage well the tension between sustaining a tradition and guiding innovation toward new initiatives. The skills to maintain and improve ongoing ministries while exploring and implementing new ministries are crucial. Leaders needed today for the new church face the reality that not only does leadership require both efforts, but the two endeavors require different skills. These skills will be explored and illustrated as we move forward in the book.

Pitting established programs against new initiatives rarely produces change, however. Ongoing operations and ministries cannot and should not be allowed to languish as bold new ventures arise because ongoing traditions often provide continuity and assets that make innovation possible. In fact, the "way things are" that leaders so frequently react against may be among the greatest assets leaders have to move into the future. These assets are often easy to take for granted. Just think about what some of them might be:

- People. Maybe they are not as many, as young, as diverse, or as future-oriented as we would like, but people's absence, for the most part, would not strengthen the church.
- Money. Maybe it is not as available as we would like, but still, without money, the church would be weaker.
- Facilities. Maybe they are not in great shape or configured for the future, but all things being equal, it is better to have facilities than to not have them.
- Culture. Maybe it is not as healthy or forward-looking as we might like, but we need a culture to carry change, and rarely is a culture so devoid of potential that values and themes from history cannot be a bridge from what is to what is needed.
- Reputation. Maybe we don't have the best reputation, but being a known entity in the community can establish credibility and open doors.
- Systems. Maybe they are not as efficient and productive as you might like, but staying connected to existing systems to help carry a vision for the future can be more worthwhile than starting from scratch.
- Staff and volunteers. Maybe they are not as gifted, energetic, or cooperative as you may wish, but if

change is needed going forward, they provide an established base from which to bring it about.

- Programs. Maybe the efforts are not exactly what is needed and perhaps are not going as well as they might, but new leaders need to resist the temptation to view what is happening upon their arrival as ordinary compared to new ideas that are innovative.

You can easily see that sustaining leadership is as necessary as innovative leadership. Each can help and support the other. And a leader can show no favorites because together, sustaining and innovative efforts are essential for a church's future. The church needs the fruits of both sustaining and innovative leadership, and neither can replace or be practiced to the exclusion of the other if a church is to enhance ministry in a productive way. But as we will see throughout this book, the two realities of sustaining leadership and innovative leadership are distinct, requiring different approaches and different skills.

DIFFERENT LEADERS FOR DIFFERENT SEASONS

Since the beginning point for leadership is not the leader but rather the people God has given the leader to work with, the leader's personal preferences for such things as worship and programs matter less than the needs of the congregation at this time in their history. One implication of this principle is that there is no rule of thumb dictating what proportion of a leader's effort should be dedicated to sustaining leadership versus innovative leadership. But we know that the historical and contextual season of a church's life will be a key factor in how effective leaders apportion their energy. Churches go through seasons in their lifetimes just as individuals do. The early years are far different from a season of maturity built on decades of lay and clergy accomplishments. Times of decline in their surrounding constituency bring challenges far different from times of growth in their surrounding population.

Gothic Church started in the 1920s, well before people began moving beyond the heart of the city. In those early days, this upstart church focused on a geographic area with few residents, and some people began to see another ministry field emerging. The congregation had few people or resources and certainly no permanent building of their own in their first years. There was little to sustain but much need for innovative leadership. Virtually all energy went toward the new. There were weekly worship leaders to recruit, neighbors to be visited, guests to follow up with, and church structures to establish. Today, one hundred years later, this church has not only its own building but an awe-inspiring one at that. It has one of the best locations in the city — a city whose boundaries have expanded in the intervening years. In another tradition, it might be a cathedral church. Typically, it attracts superior clergy and staff leaders and has a prosperous and dedicated membership. Today also, along with its strengths, it faces the same challenges as other tall-steeple churches with fantastic reputations but aging memberships: the population shifts people followed a century ago take them even farther from the expanded city into ever-growing suburbs. Even as new growth took place away from their church, enough of the congregation remained or commuted to the church to preserve their strength.

The pastoral leadership needs of Gothic Church have changed as the church's seasons have changed. In those early decades of the twentieth century, planning for an uncertain future required extensive and able innovative leadership. Today, the gravitational pull of such a long-standing and prestigious church is toward sustaining its ministry and mission. Gothic Church's noteworthy characteristics and programs merit respect, and the congregation can well expect them to continue. However, in these early decades of the twenty-first century, much has changed in the context and surroundings of Gothic Church. Its future will require finding effective and faithful ways to adapt to these changing times and circumstances. The easiest thing for a pastoral leader to do at Gothic Church is to focus exclusively on sustaining leadership. The needed and more difficult task, however, is to provide innovative leadership; and yet, in these new circumstances, there can be no innovative leadership unless there is sufficient attention to sustaining leadership. All that has provided a strong foundation for Gothic Church through the years must continue to undergird its ministry: the faithful and generous people, the creative and effective programs, and the congregational governance and structures that have enabled this ministry. All these strengths must be nurtured and sustained. Otherwise, there will be no grounding for the innovation that will help shape their next faithful step in ministry.

Contemporary Church is in the same city. In the early decades of the twentieth century, when Gothic Church was struggling to shape its ministry in a newly developing part of the city, our second church was located in an area of the central city where things were established and stable. A population of working people who were rearing their families surrounded Contemporary Church. This church was not worrying about whether anyone would come to worship each week. Members of the solid, dependable, close-knit church family faithfully carried out their responsibilities. After a few decades, a new pastor arrived and faced as many expectations for sustaining leadership as a pastor at Gothic Church faces today. The preaching, teaching, and pastoral care needs of the church could easily fill the new pastor's time. While the desire of the congregation was for sustaining leadership to take prominence, the new pastor came to see that innovative leadership was the true need. The community was changing. No longer was it as desirable a community for newcomers. Those with sufficient resources were moving to the suburbs, far beyond where Gothic Church had established itself. In their place came new people who were different from the church's all-white, middle-class constituency. Like the longtime residents, they were hardworking but enjoyed fewer good job options and faced more hurdles.

The new pastor, who had come to Contemporary Church at the time of these significant population changes, had a lengthy and thriving pastorate. It began with the necessity of innovative leadership in light of the rapidly changing context of the community. When the previous pastor of Contemporary Church retired after thirty years of ministry there, the church that once had a few hundred members now had thousands, and half the participants were people of color. It was now time for another pastor to serve Contemporary Church. The pastor observed the progress made by this congregation over three decades in an area where dozens of churches had closed or relocated during that time of radical community change. This pastor wisely discerned that sustaining leadership had to be offered in a way that allowed for innovative leadership. For one reason, the community's race and age demographics were continuing to change and were increasingly different from those of the current multiracial congregation. The leadership of the pastor during this chapter of Contemporary Church's story gave attention to the sustaining work needed so that the people were open to the innovation that also was required. Today the church reflects those innovations, having now a strong majority of people of color, primarily African American, and focusing on the growth of a younger constituency among their five thousand–plus worshippers.

Today if you drove by Gothic Church and Contemporary Church, you would notice similarities. Both have impressive, though different, physical structures. The first is English Gothic with cathedral-like stone towers, while the second is contemporary with lots of glass, more like a convention center than a cathedral. Both are large compared to other churches in their traditions and are known by most leaders within their denominations. Yet they have traveled different paths. Their beginnings shaped who they are today. Initially, pastors of Gothic Church had to provide primarily innovative leadership. Success led to greater needs for sustaining leadership to a point that sustaining leadership was assumed by established congregational leaders to be the natural role for pastors. Yet this new season of the church's life, a century after it first began and hence surrounded by a new context, called for innovative leadership as creative as at its beginning. Such innovation differed from those first years, since now leaders were called to honor and build on a rich heritage while guiding the congregation into a new era. In Contemporary Church, what appeared to be a church needing (certainly wanting and expecting) sustaining leadership turned out to be one whose very existence, much less growth, depended on decades of innovative leadership through multiple changes in its context and community. Sustaining and innovating leadership are never to be seen in isolation but will have a rhythm that depends on where a congregation is in its life and the ways in which its context is changing.

A RHYTHM OF SUSTAINING AND INNOVATING LEADERSHIP

Tradition is not the past; it is the perennial extension of well-grounded life into the future. Tradition is the activity of living in the present in full connection with all the past that has brought it into being.

—Craig Dykstra, "Deep Veins of Wisdom"

A pastor in Florida recounts that in his early years as a pastor, one of his mentors reminded him that the roots of the church had been established long before he got there and would hopefully continue to grow long after he was gone. His mentor encouraged him to tend the vine so that it could continue to bear fruit in the future. The pastor reports quickly learning that "tending the vine is not always easy, especially when the act of pruning becomes inevitable."[2] Established vineyards (churches) have likely been tilled by countless others before you. You might be acutely aware of planting that did not fit the climate or required far too much labor given the fruit produced. You see daily the parts of the vineyard regularly neglected over the years. Humility comes from knowing that you too will make similar, if different, mistakes during your tenure. So without any sense of moral or leadership superiority, you provide sustaining leadership that builds on the best of the past, as flawed as it may be, with the profound awareness, as Craig Dykstra puts it, "that present, past, and future are upheld by the everlasting arms of God."[3]

It is sustaining leadership that makes possible innovative leadership, but it is insufficient by itself. Navigating the leadership horizon today requires both types of leadership and the wisdom to know which is needed when and in what proportions. Both always need to be on your mind and shape all your words and actions. Drawing upon the familiar dynamics of your congregation's patterns or the comfortable scope of your leadership practices will not suffice in today's challenging environment filled with new and unfamiliar issues.

In some ways, this leadership challenge illustrates Ronald Heifetz's distinction between technical and adaptive challenges mentioned earlier. Leaders face both challenges. Leaders do not get to choose which types of challenges to address. And remember Heifetz's warning that the biggest mistake a leader can make is to treat an adaptive challenge as a technical challenge. So discernment about what requires true sustaining leadership and what must be addressed through innovative leadership is critical.

The first step for leaders wishing to make a difference in their congregation's effectiveness in fulfilling its mission is to acknowledge that their churches are the incumbents, with all the strengths and drawbacks that go with that status. Churches are often among the legacy institutions of the community. Though they may be weaker than before, they are hardly marginal organizations. They have histories, traditions, and reputations in the community. Leaders, therefore, have a responsibility to provide sustaining leadership to carry forth those strengths and that foundation. It is from this base, then, that they look forward to faithfully carrying out new callings that will be shaped by innovative leadership.

Sustaining and innovative leadership are not to be seen as in conflict or as if one is preferable to the other. Each has its place in the seasons and changes in a congregation's life and in the attentiveness required to account for the changing contexts surrounding the congregation. Sustaining and innovative leadership live in a rhythm. Both are required if a congregation is to take those next faithful steps to which God always calls us.

Chapter 3

The Opportunities and Limitations of Sustaining Leadership

Let's look to an example outside the church to see the opportunities and limitations of sustaining leadership. Suppose you are the new director of Community Blood Bank. This is not your first experience with blood banks. You have worked in several previously, including a successful tenure at a similar, though smaller, blood bank in the same state. You know the universe of blood banks well and are familiar with standards and best practices.

GETTING STARTED

As an experienced leader, you know that you need to listen before talking, so you begin your tenure in conversation with many people. You have your questions ready. Every encounter is a chance to learn information that you will need to lead.

You begin by asking the most basic of questions: "What is the purpose of Community Blood Bank?" or "What is the mission of Community Blood Bank?" You are pleasantly surprised to learn that the blood bank has a clearly stated mission, and most people seem to know it well. It is found regularly on organization documents and is posted prominently in its facilities. The purpose statement is as follows: "Community Blood Bank exists so that sufficient safe blood components and services are provided to local hospitals to meet the needs of our community." While the statement could be fine-tuned a bit, you think there is no need to do so at this time. You are grateful that there is a mission, and based on your conversation, you believe people understand the core purpose of the organization.

Next you inquire about the values of Community Blood Bank. While a purpose statement lays out an organization's goal, effective ones identify core values that serve as boundaries within which they choose to operate. Organizations that name their values say, in effect, "We are not willing to do just anything to achieve our goal. Our daily practices are guided by these shared values." So you ask about the values of Community Blood Bank. Again, you are pleased that those with whom you talk know exactly what you have in mind. In fact, you see throughout the building a nice poster that outlines the core values Community Blood Bank intends to exemplify as it achieves its purpose.

You quickly look over the chart and see words associated with values common among blood banks, such as *inclusive*, *nondiscriminatory*, *confidentiality*, *safety*, *welcoming*, *appreciative*, *accountable*, and *transparent*, among others. You are not so concerned about the exact language, as you are happy to see that yet another foundational component of a successful organization is in place.

Now it is time to learn more about the inner workings. This is where mission and values are embodied in policies and daily practices. You are eager to learn how things work here and what others see as strengths and challenges. You begin with the organizational chart, which shows all the departments and the staff person responsible for each. You set times to meet with these unit leaders. You tell them you want to hear about their overall annual plans and procedures to accomplish their part of the mission and then what things they do very well and areas that need to improve.

ONE MONTH LATER

This process takes several weeks. You talk with those most responsible for blood collection, processing, testing, storage, outreach, finance, human resources, facilities, and other aspects of the organization's work. You learn a lot. You are taking notes and, in the process, forming a to-do list for your first year. In addition to your questions, staff are sharing information about themselves and others, such as plans to retire or to move away. More tasks for your list! They also share their assessments of the work of colleagues in their department or other areas. You will need more information to evaluate what you are hearing.

At the same time you are listening to staff leaders, you are also engaged in daily conversations with others who work for the blood bank — volunteers and members of the community at large. From chats with neighbors to conversations with members of the board of directors, you are gathering important clues about community perceptions and opinions. The questions you are asked after a civic club presentation tell what is on the minds of those not connected daily to the organization. You add information from these encounters to your notes and, in some cases, to your task list. They certainly give you new lines of inquiry as you meet with staff.

After all these formal and informal sessions, you understand the current situation of the blood bank you are leading in a far more complete and nuanced way than when you arrived a month before. You had an impression of this blood bank before you accepted the position based on reports and word of mouth about blood banks in the state. Now some of those impressions are confirmed, but many more are not. Everything seemed so simple when you arrived. There were a few issues that everyone knew needed attention. Now even those issues turn out not to be as clear-cut as most assume, and they involve a complex set of variables not immediately visible to an outside observer.

Now, after a month on duty, you, as the new blood bank director, have a long list of tasks for the next year. The tasks include a mixture of simple items requiring little effort and complex matters requiring major changes to policies, structure, personnel, or culture. The list needs categorizing and prioritizing. Soon the director creates a new list with an order and neatness belying the magnitude of the challenge. It covers the small technical changes for which there is consensus—tasks requiring less work. Some of these items will turn out to be surprisingly hard to change, but for the most part, these can be handled with little effort or drama.

You focus attention each day on issues related to handling and distributing the blood as well as matters of governance, personnel, finance, and outreach. For some categories, the to-do list is long; for others, it is much shorter. But now you have a self-imposed mandate to make Community Blood Bank better.

ONE YEAR LATER

A small celebration is held to recognize your first anniversary as director of Community Blood Bank. Some staff have decorated a room used for staff meetings with balloons. You receive a nice card signed by all the staff. A few of the more senior unit leaders highlight some of the progress made in your first year. You are appropriately surprised and humbled and then remind everyone that it is time to get back to work to keep the progress going.

When you return to your office, you pull up on your computer that all too familiar task list developed eleven months ago. It now reflects weekly or sometimes daily updates from the past months. You remember how overwhelming the list appeared at the beginning. You had thought of it as a checklist that, with enough time and work, would become shorter as you completed project after project. In one sense, that is how it worked. You feel good remembering the many tasks addressed successfully and their removal from the list.

However, the list did not shrink as you had anticipated. For every task completed, another seemed to appear. The personnel change you made because of a staff member's lack of technical competence resulted in hiring someone who had all the knowledge and skills required for the role. Unfortunately, the new person could not work with others and had little interest in doing so. A new task was added. The leader of another department that presented few problems because of their good work told you this morning about a family relocation, a move producing a vacancy for the blood bank. Another task is added. The new safety protocols have received high marks, but now hospitals are complaining about longer wait times for blood. One more task added.

OPPORTUNITIES

There is a saying that when one is interviewed for a leadership position, they learn about a quarter of the issues facing the organization. When they are hired, they are told another quarter of the issues. The remaining 50 percent they have to learn on their own! By now, you can no doubt see many parallels between the experiences of this blood bank director and those of a new leader for a congregation or other setting. Things go from simple to complex quickly. New tasks emerge faster than old tasks are completed as the leader learns more about the situation.

This managerial aspect of the leader's role will not change dramatically year after year. Ideally others will come to share new standards, and gradually an improved culture will develop so that others handle many problems before they get to the leader, or they never occur at all. The benefits of this leadership are sustaining in that they build on the basic assumptions of the organization and practices that have been done before but not at the new levels of performance. Things will improve, but problems will not go away. Rather, the problems will move to a higher level. There will still be financial issues, for example, but now they are more likely to involve deciding where a new staff position should go from increased funding rather than deciding which position to eliminate because of financial shortfalls. That is progress itself.

Returning to the blood bank, for example, in the early days, it was difficult to get anyone to serve on the board of directors. Years later, the reputation of the organization and the quality of its directors have changed. Now you still face annual challenges around board membership. However, your effort goes into selecting among numerous potential candidates and making sure these equally qualified potential members will add to the various types of diversity and experience needed for effective board work.

Even after just one year, it is obvious to you and those in the blood bank world who have a basis for judging its performance that Community Blood Bank is a more viable organization and is implementing its mission more effectively than a year before. There is no reason to expect that this will change. Year after year, things should get better. In fact, as proud as you are of the achievements of the first year and as difficult as many (even small) improvements were to make, you will make progress in five or more years that you and your colleagues cannot imagine now. The hard work in the early years on seemingly small things makes greater achievements possible later. There is indeed a virtuous cycle when good leadership is present.

Now picture yourself ten years after beginning as director of Community Blood Bank. A splendid banquet is held to celebrate the progress of Community Blood Bank during your directorship. You are preparing to leave this assignment to take on another position, one offered to you primarily because of the record you established over the past decade. Your contributions to the community are well known and appreciated. The community wants to say "thank you" in a special way. The program is well planned. In succinct presentations, speaker after speaker names specific achievements during your tenure that show how the functioning of the blood bank and, with it, the lives of those in the community served by Community Blood Bank have improved. A beautiful plaque is presented to a standing ovation from the crowded banquet hall.

LIMITATIONS

As important as the sustaining leadership demonstrated in this example is, a multitude of limitations arise when a leader focuses only on sustaining.

Let's take the best-case scenario: the context stays relatively stable during a leader's tenure. There are no major disruptions from the economy, competition, or scandals. In such favorable circumstances, the managerial achievements should come more easily, and the likelihood that they remain in place is high. What may be missed by a leader in such an environment is the need to address a major adaptive challenge not on the minds of staff or directors. The leader missed it because shared basic assumptions within the organization kept it off the radar. Shared basic assumptions are those things written nowhere but that shape daily activities more powerfully than any mission statement, posted values, or board actions. The limitations of such assumptions cause organizations to miss the "elephant in the room"—the major challenge that can never be addressed by incremental management improvements.

So in addition to the significant work of sustaining and improving what is, leaders must also look for what's missing. In our scenario, apart from sustaining improvements, what is Community Blood Bank called to do in this chapter of its history that will require new learning and a new way of thinking about who we are and what we are called to do—that will require innovating? The leader is constantly asking the question, "Given our purpose and our context (internal and external), what is Community Blood Bank called to do in the near future?" We use *near future* knowing that the appropriate time horizon for this next step varies considerably by groups and their circumstances.

Now consider a less than ideal scenario in which multiple disruptions occur during the leader's tenure. Income declines, a safety breach alarms the community, and there is high staff turnover. Even through all these challenges, a director who provides solid, sustaining leadership will usually get high marks. However, with or without disruptions in an organization's context, a leader might miss opportunities to make even more important contributions due to an exclusive, though noteworthy, focus on sustaining leadership.

Here is an example from Community Blood Bank. With all the good work in their history and the improvements guided by their most recent leader, there was an adaptive challenge never addressed. An issue that is never discussed or questioned (remember the power of unstated basic assumptions) but becomes immediately evident to an outside observer with any knowledge of the community is that from its start, the blood bank, despite its name, has served primarily one portion of the community. The bank is located in a part of the community with a distinct racial and cultural makeup, and all of its activities seem to be focused on serving that demographic. Other parts of the community that are more diverse rarely factor into leadership, staff, or plans. All directors come from one part of the community. All the volunteer organizations and churches with which the blood bank has alliances are located in that same part of the community.

In addition to improvements in virtually every arena of its internal work that needed to be made upon the arrival of the new director ten years ago, another more basic leadership need was apparent. Community Blood Bank needed to live up to its name and become "Community Blood Bank for the whole community." Achieving this goal requires a level of leadership and innovation for which the sustaining leadership tool kit is inadequate.

The tendency in mature congregations is to improve the "performance" of each of their ministry areas. Leaders celebrate the opportunity to improve God's work through this church and contribute to the faith development of many people through these ministries. Improvements through such good management do indeed advance the mission of the church. But there are limits to good management, and most churches have run up against them in recent decades. This is when churches have discovered that good practices, even superior practices, are no longer good enough.

No matter how laity and clergy change or improve ministries, the impact of those ministries continues to decline. The problem is that the assumptions on which the ministries were founded and now continue no longer fit the context of the congregation. Leadership requires more than doing things well. Many declining churches are very accomplished and carry out their ministries conscientiously. Doing things well is far better than not doing them well, of course, but something more is required for congregations to be vital.

Chapter 4

The Leader as Sustainer

Established congregations have a dynamic far different from that of new congregations. A new church's survival depends on an outward focus that establishes relationships within the community. Virtually all energy goes toward making those connections that are essential to establishing a cadre of engaged participants who form the core group for the new church. In all fairness, clergy and laity in new churches can devote themselves to these outreach efforts because compared to established congregations, they have fewer sustaining responsibilities. The new church is too small to have many pastoral needs, and the educational, mission, and governance structures are in their infancy. Worship is a high priority because its quality is a major factor in determining whether first-time guests return. Even as programs and ministries begin beyond worship, the outward focus on reaching new people is paramount. The decision, in the first place, that there is a need for a new congregation requires that the newly formed church move forward to reach new people. New churches that do not establish strong connections with the larger community have difficulty becoming strong and vital congregations.

The need for more internal attention grows with every new program, class, and ministry, along with the greater pastoral care needs that come with a congregation much larger than it was in its first few years. Leaders in such churches gradually find that their ongoing responsibilities for existing people and programs take most of their time and energy to begin stabilizing a foundation for this new congregation. Such ministry is different from the work of leaders in long-established congregations, however, where current members and ministries receive the bulk of the attention.

After a time, if the new church grows stronger and some consider a need for innovation, a pastor cannot simply take for granted the current congregation's ministries and expect them to stay in place and take care of themselves while also leading the church in bold new ventures. Change does not happen that way. Effective leaders, even visionary leaders, recognize that innovation and revitalization require both sustaining leadership and innovative leadership.

In this chapter, we focus on sustaining leadership, which supports the daily work and established patterns of congregations. This work, particularly building on the strengths of the congregation and minimizing its weaknesses, is preparation for innovating. Even incremental change, made collectively as a result of efforts to sustain, can be as powerful in its own way as innovative leadership. Although they cannot rely on sustaining leadership alone to change the trajectory of their church in ways that align with today's social context, leaders need first to understand and develop the skills needed to faithfully and effectively sustain ministry.

THE BIG AND DAILY THINGS

Before all else, leaders—whether sustaining or innovating—must earn the right to lead people where they are not asking to go. Church leadership, especially that which goes beyond what people have known, requires that a congregation trust their pastor. Their leader must have credibility. Some credibility comes by virtue of a leader's office but not nearly as much as leaders often assume. At times, a leader enters their role as pastoral leader with a reputation of character and competence. That reputation may suffice for a time, but ongoing credibility results from a leader illustrating character and competence day by day in the life of the congregation. It grows from building relationships that demonstrate the trust required to lead the people God has given this pastor to serve.

Good sustaining leadership provides excellent opportunities for developing the trust that people require before more innovative leadership efforts can be considered or initiated. Therefore, a leader's priorities need to align with those things that are most needed by the congregation in this season of sustaining.

So what does a congregation most need? Wise leaders do not answer this question with a list of things that need to be changed. They begin by asking the right questions, even when they have few answers. Two such questions fit as they are deciding what ongoing ministries require sustained attention, no matter what new initiatives may emerge:

- What does every participant in a congregation have a right to expect from their church?
- What do they have a right to expect from their leader?

The answers to these questions have little to do with what people "want" or survey results. They are more basic than that. These questions push us to those most fundamental responsibilities of a church and its pastoral leaders that fair-minded, objective observers could agree people have a right to expect. Disregarding these basic expectations can destroy the foundation of trust and confidence people need in order to explore more innovative ventures. Some of the struggles of congregations today may have as much to do with neglecting these responsibilities as they do with not taking on the changing context.

Whatever an innovation will involve, the influence and work of a few key leaders, especially those who have certain governance responsibilities, will be essential to success. However, no major new effort can ultimately succeed without the cooperation, not necessarily agreement or even participation, of a whole range of stakeholder groups that have common interests and often common connections with one another. They may not embody the future direction of the church, but they can derail change efforts if they are disregarded, their interests are devalued, and their basic needs are not addressed.

So what are those basics that must receive unfaltering attention?

A SPIRITUAL GROUNDING

A congregation does many things, but its focus is always on knowing God and doing God's will. People can abide disappointments with their church, but a lively and ongoing experience of God's presence is essential to any congregation and its constituents. If this source of power flickers or comes into doubt, few good things are likely to happen. It is from a powerful relationship to the spirit of Christ that all else flows. The spiritual grounding of a congregation can never be assumed. It must be explicit, so no one doubts the source of all ministries and all endeavors.

Leaders must embody this spiritual grounding and communicate it with energy and consistency. Effective leaders are known for their commitment to the vision God has given the congregation they serve and to the discerning of the next faithful steps God has for the church. Members of struggling churches often have trouble identifying why their church is different from other churches or what distinctive contribution God expects of them. Members of growing churches believe God has given them a special calling in their communities, although such a belief does not devalue other congregations, which are assumed also to have a distinct calling from God.

VITAL WORSHIP

Worship—gathering to glorify God and share God as revealed in Jesus Christ—is the reason any church exists. The church is much more than worship, but without vital worship, it is unlikely that members are growing and new disciples are being reached. When a church's worship is not vital, almost every other aspect of the congregation's ministry is hampered. Vital churches today spend far more time on worship planning, preparation, and evaluation than struggling churches do. Worship is not everything the church does, but it is primary, and other ministries flow from it.[1]

Sometimes, however, worship—and all that goes into its preparation, execution, and evaluation—is seen as but one of many responsibilities claiming a leader's time. That is not how either longtime members or new guests view worship. It stands above other things, partly because it is the experience most church attenders typically share. In fact, worship, particularly preaching and music, often takes on even greater importance for the average member than for the most active member. If worship slips in vitality, the most active members may still connect with their faith communities in many other ways, particularly through multiple and strong personal relationships. On the other hand, less active members may be the first to complain or, even worse, to worship less frequently because of a congregation's inadequate focus on worship. If a church, even one in decline, succeeds in reaching more people in worship, then a different church emerges and is on its way to a new day.

ATTENTION TO THE PEOPLE

Without people, there is no congregation. Yet while most leaders think their efforts are for the benefit of others, many people do not feel included in the community of faith. That is one of the dangers of leading from an insider's way of thinking, or what we call "inside-to-outside thinking." Such thinking focuses on what the leaders of the congregation—clergy and lay—plan for the congregation and then offers these plans to the larger congregation for their participation. These leaders fail to give attention to what those beyond the insiders are hearing—and especially the ways in which those new to the congregation may feel like outsiders.

When new people join our churches, we promise to support and care for them. We sometimes use family language to stress that all members are held together by bonds comparable to those of a healthy family. Do we really mean that? If a sibling or cousin misses family events where they normally would be present, does anyone notice? I think so. Yet people can feel lost so easily within this community of faith where people have vowed to care for one another.

Paying attention to one another is a spiritual discipline to be cultivated within a congregation and modeled by its leaders. A congregation is called to genuinely pay attention to those around them. Each member, new or longtime, can expect others to notice their presence or absence. They can anticipate that their joys and concerns, spoken aloud in prayer or whispered to a worshipping neighbor, will draw expressions of care from others. Leaders must ensure this happens by modeling personal attention and concern and also by nourishing a culture, including structures for providing care, that pays attention to all those God has given to the congregation.

We spoke previously about how crucial it is to ask what people have a right to expect from their leaders. The first steps we have described are to make sure we are meeting the rightful spiritual and pastoral expectations of the congregation. Many people become inactive and disconnected from the congregation when there seems no longer to be a lively and ongoing experience of God's presence in the worship and mission life of the church. Therefore, the primacy of vital and always improving worship is essential. Also crucial, then, is a call arising from worship to grow in discipleship and reach out in mission and service to others.

Often, it seems, both longtime members and those new to the congregation receive the message that people are there to support the church. They may hear leaders emphasizing those programs and events that insiders have decided are important. What if leaders assumed a different stance in approaching their congregations? "How can we help you grow in your discipleship journey?" might be a good place to start. We could say, "Our task is to help you grow in your walk with God and deepen your relationship with Christ. We want to make sure you have what you need to take your next faithful step." Leaders would then focus on what we call "outside-to-inside thinking." They would ask questions and listen, and they would develop the kinds of events and programs that help the congregation grow in their walk with God. Out of these ministries, people of faith could then deepen their relationships with Christ through study and devotional practices of which they may not have been aware. They would be strengthened to join ministries of mission, outreach, and justice. Sustaining leaders thus focus on maintaining a sense of God's presence in the life of the congregation and the call to each person to grow in their relationship with Christ.

Sustaining leaders will also ensure that effective pastoral and congregational care take place. People have a right to expect those forms of ministry in their congregations. No one person can be expected to address all the concerns for care in the church. While church members will rightly expect pastoral care, each congregation must develop an effective system of congregational care based on strong networks, relationships, and structures. Longtime members and those new to a church should not have to question whether their presence or their well-being matters to the church. Unfortunately, most churches have better structures for keeping track of who does or does not contribute financially than who is or is not present in other ministries to the extent that they once might have been. We must find ways to ensure the pastoral and congregational care that our people deserve so they can and will remain the active and faithful participants we pray they will be.

People join churches for various reasons, but most stay involved because of relationships. When pastors and staff are asked why people participate in their churches, they name worship, pastors, music, and programs. But when congregants are asked, they tend to talk about their connections with others. Finding effective ways for people to develop those relationships can become part of what holds the community together and will be an integral dimension of pastoral and congregational care that strengthens the community of faith. Together, these elements will prepare the congregation to take its next faithful steps in response to God's call upon its life.

Chapter 5

The Leader as Innovator

One of the most influential management and leadership thinkers of the past fifty years was Clayton M. Christensen, who taught at Harvard Business School. Several years ago, he wanted to discover why good companies do not stay atop their fields when confronted by certain types of change. His interest was not why a particular company failed due to some industry or company-specific weakness. Rather, he was seeking common patterns that caused good companies to lose their leadership edge as new entrants in the market did much better.

He selected the disk drive industry for study. Why disk drives? For the same reason those who study genetics study fruit flies instead of humans! A generation for a fruit fly is one day, not thirty years. The disk drive industry has gone through generations at a "fruit fly" pace. Within a relatively short time, there have been multiple generations of technology and multiple leaders in the industry.

Why is it, Christensen asked, that the dominant company in one generation of disk drive technology is virtually never the leader in the next? Conventional wisdom assumes these companies began practicing poor management, despite years of superior management practices. How else could decline be explained?

Christensen found just the opposite to be the case. Indeed, even as these companies lost their positions of market strength, their operations were exemplary. They knew their customers, listened to their customers, and focused on quality and responsiveness. Decisions were made based on solid business logic.

If these good companies had not become bad companies before declining, what did happen? He found that there is something about how decisions are made in established and successful organizations that sows the seeds of eventual failure. While traditional management is well suited to "sustaining innovation," the tools of good management are inadequate when confronted with "disruptive innovation." Sustaining innovation focuses on improving current products and services. This is particularly the case in relation to a company's best customers and the products or services from which most of their profit derives. More features are added to products, and services are expanded. These new and more complex offerings set them apart as leaders in the field who offer quality, advanced products or services. While these changes meet needs, especially for their best customers, the price to customers increases.

However, the very things that make the established companies strong also make them vulnerable to disruptive innovations. In the business world, disruptors tend to enter at the low end of offerings and target customers who do not need all the "bells and whistles" of the offerings from the established company and those for whom the related costs are not welcome. The competing product offered usually will have fewer features and will not provide the quality of the high-end competition. The disruptor's success comes from those who do not need all the features and those who could not afford (or are unwilling to pay for) the quality but still need the basic product.

For example, the emergence of discount stores was a "disruptive innovation" for department stores. What department stores did best was meet the needs of their primary constituents. They could not, at the same time, address the competition presented by the new discount stores. Everything department stores had learned about meeting the needs of their traditional customers meant that they knew little about the needs of a constituency cultivated by a new breed of retailers.

So it was with the disk drive industry. While one company perfected their technology and offerings to serve their best and most profitable customers, another company offered a scaled-down and cheaper product aimed at the lower end of the market. The losses for the established company were minimal, but this lower-grade product continued to improve. As this happened, more customers who could afford (or were now willing to pay for) the more expensive offerings of the incumbent company decided the new company's products were good for them as well. The once dominant company did not regain its leadership in the market.

Similarly, the early discount stores received little attention from department stores because the new stores were serving a new constituency—lower-income people—who rarely shopped at department stores anyway. Furthermore, the locations, displays, and merchandise in discount stores had little to offer the traditional department store customers. However, as time went by, the discount stores did not stay the same. As is usually the case with disruptive innovations, they first attracted the unserved or underserved. The clothes may be stacked on tables with narrow aisles, and there may be no staff to help customers. But that did not deter persons with little money to spend from shopping at a place seemingly built for them. No atmosphere but low, low prices. As time goes by, the discount stores evolve. Now the stores are a bit brighter, aisles a bit wider, and displays sorted by brands and sizes. Also, new customers now come from a broader spectrum of the population. Many people who could pay department store prices now do at least a portion of their shopping at discount stores.

The same phenomenon happened in the automobile industry. New carmakers from other countries entered the US market, offering smaller cars that competed with US car makers at the lowest end of both the cost scale for consumers and the profit scale for manufacturers. Seeing little threat to the heart of their business economic models, the US larger car manufacturers paid little attention to the new entrants in the marketplace. Today, many of those newer carmakers compete directly with established US firms in all categories of cars, including the most expensive and highest quality ones. The disruptive innovation represented by this new competition gave no signs of such strength in the early days. They improved and expanded the quality and variety of their offerings. They expanded the base of customers who took them quite seriously when they were selecting a new car to purchase.

MEANING FOR CHURCHES

"What in the world could all this mean for churches?" you may be asking. We do not want to belabor Christensen's idea of disruptive innovation but want to highlight the ways these points apply to congregations.

We can see elements of disruptive innovation going on in the Protestant Reformation. Martin Luther's challenge to the established church was indeed disruptive and reached many unserved or underserved people, a key characteristic of disruptive innovation. Among Luther's early theses was his conviction that laity, not only the clergy and the pope, had a significant place in the church. He also named the primacy of faith rather than good works in our salvation—and thus opposed the system of indulgences by which money had to be paid for "forgiveness." Indulgences were theologically unsound, and they put excessive pressure on the poor. We see another example in England with the Wesleyan movement. As in Luther's era, one church was dominant; in this second case, it was the Church of England. The Wesleyan Revival introduced "disruptive innovations" such as field preaching, class meetings, and lay preachers. In both examples, the response of the established church was to ignore, criticize, or ridicule these new ideas. Surely there was no reason for such powerful institutions to worry, since the upstart movements were neither thought to be legitimate nor seen as a threat to their power and position in the society.

Or take the situation of mainline churches in the United States over the past half century or more. These denominations functioned virtually as the nation's established church for a long time. Presidents met with their leaders, and national commissions included their representatives. But things began to change, and some of those changes came from what appear now to be disruptive innovations. Changes included different music and worship styles, informality, less traditional church buildings, and leaders from a broad spectrum of society whose formal credentials received less attention.

Think of yourself as a leader in First Mainline Church on the town square just across from the courthouse, a church with many political, business, and social leaders in the community as members. You are highly educated, and the church staff are all trained and certified in their fields of work. The music director heads the music department at a local college. Not only is your church the oldest in the county, but it also has one of the most imposing physical structures in town. You were very proud to become pastor of First Church. It is thought of within your judicatory as one of the strong churches. However, while there are no financial difficulties, and members see the church as strong as always, you have identified troubling trends. Beginning decades ago, levels of attendance and overall participation have consistently gone down year after year. The number of children and youth is embarrassingly low. But none of these trends diminishes the pride that members have in their church and its assumed good future.

In the church library, you come across a history of the community from 1965, when the church was celebrating its centennial. A whole chapter is devoted to religious life. The chapter begins with the story of First Church, the first congregation established even before the town officially incorporated. You learn of the church's modest beginning but fast growth through a combination of evangelical zeal and a growing population. The history includes pictures of previous locations and buildings before the church relocated to its current prominent location in 1956. Then the other churches are described in their order of establishment. All of them are still active. You consider them all "brother/sister" churches, since their traditions are quite compatible with yours. All the pastors belong to the ecumenical clergy fellowship, and several joint services and outreach efforts continue. No other churches are discussed, but you must assume there were others in existence by the 1960s.

Reading this chapter gives you the idea of comparing the religious landscape then and now. The town history gives you valuable information to form a baseline against which to compare the current situation. You quickly are struck by the changes. In the 1970s, the tiny Nazarene church that worshipped in a small building in town relocated to a newly forming subdivision. They purchased a great deal of land and, over the years, developed an impressive church campus, the largest in the county. Today, the Nazarene church is the largest church in the area. In the 1980s, a Pentecostal church began meeting in a closed furniture store. When they outgrew that space, they moved to an elementary school. Then they built a prefab steel building a few miles from town. They are now the second-largest church in the county.

When you ask some of your church members about these two churches, since they were established after the town history was written, the members do not seem to know much about them. In some cases, they have neighbors who attend these churches. You soon discover that some families that have been members of First Church for generations are now worshipping there. They left First Church reluctantly and with no bad feelings. Their children were attracted to the focus on youth ministry at the other churches, and the parents decided to join them, thrilled to see their children's enthusiasm.

Others you talk to comment on the "types" of people who attend these churches and their pastors' and staff's lack of "proper" credentials. Some assume that, surely, they are compromising sound theology if they are attracting so many who never had gone to church before. But they all admit that these newer churches work hard and seem to meet the needs of the people who worship there.

You begin to consider what people experience in those churches compared to the long-established churches so prominently described in the town's centennial history. Instead of ushers waiting inside to greet and give bulletins to those arriving, the newer churches have greeters outside and even ushers in the parking lots. The energy level and the sound of the music are certainly much higher than at First Church. Dress is much more casual than it is for your members. The sermon topics appear more practical.

As much as the large number of people attending these newer churches must appreciate those distinctive features, they still have little appeal to leaders at First Church. For several years, the congregation discussed relocating but finally decided it just would not be First Church if it were not in the center of the town. Likewise, younger members had pushed for more "contemporary" music. The worship committee met with music leaders and held focus groups with members but finally concluded that the music is a distinctive characteristic of First Church. There was also reluctance by the worship committee to offer multiple worship services, since they felt that would divide the congregation.

The established churches that were in town at the time of the centennial did not, in the next fifty or so years, become bad churches. In many ways, those churches have become stronger today than they were through sustaining improvements across the years. They have better facilities, more educated pastors and staff, and larger budgets (even after taking inflation into account), and they give more to mission than ever before. But despite all these advances through incremental progress, they no longer serve memberships as large as they did at the centennial. Their membership proportions of the community have declined even more so. They no longer have the influence within the community that they once did.

While First Church was improving on its strengths, those same strengths plus its illustrious history and reputation seemed to prevent it from doing what was required to respond to the disruptions around it. It could have done what some other churches did. It could have relocated. It could have expanded its youth program or offered different forms of worship through alternative services. Or perhaps it could have created a second campus in the area where new people were moving and let it develop with its own culture to fit that younger constituency. The downtown campus would be free to continue with the forms most comfortable and meaningful to their traditional constituency.

It was as if everything it meant for them to be "First Church" made it virtually impossible for them to respond to the disruptions. So it was in John Wesley's time that the Church of England had vast resources they could have used to start small groups or outdoor services or to experiment with more popular music. But what it meant to be the Church of England made that impossible. It was similar to the department stores that had resources to compete with discount stores, but everything they understood themselves to be made that impossible.

Christensen uses another example from the business world. Motorola originally had the rights to what became the first transistor radios. Motorola had made its name in radios in the pretelevision era, when the highest form of home entertainment was the large table radio. Families would gather to listen to their favorite radio shows just as they would later for television shows. A major source of pride for Motorola was the quality of their radios' sound. They worked hard to offer top-of-the-line table radios with constantly improving sound quality. Their goal was for a musical performance heard on the radio to sound the same as if one was in the concert hall for the performance. That meant that their best radios cost more than others, but their best customers were glad to pay for the quality and prestige of these radios with the latest features Motorola offered.

In the Motorola world of that time, there seemed to be no place for transistor technology. It had advantages, but not where it mattered to Motorola—sound quality. There was no way a transistor radio could come close to producing the sound that people expected from Motorola. They decided to sell the transistor rights. The rest is history, as people say. Just as Motorola concluded, the first transistor radios had poor sound quality compared to virtually any other radios on the market. But it turned out that there was a market for transistor radios. They did not replace table radios, but they served several constituencies that Motorola's table radios could never serve. There were many people who could not afford table radios but could afford cheap transistor radios. There was also a market among those who may already have had a table radio, even if not Motorola's top brand. They now had a radio they could take to the beach, on walks and runs, and where there was no electrical source. They knew the sound would not be perfect, but the trade-off—a radio that was so portable and versatile—overcame the sound quality issue. Notice also that the transistor radio did not remain the same. The quality, including the sound, became better, and new models, sizes, and designs were introduced, including more advanced versions that sold for higher prices and produced more profits.

INNOVATION AMID CHANGING CIRCUMSTANCES

The Motorola example shows how an organization can continue to improve what it does well while missing even greater opportunities to unfold in their changing environments. The church world resembles the business world but is also distinct from it. In both, there are basic concepts of innovation that should not be ignored. First, insiders must have an awareness of what is happening in the culture around them. It is easy to become comfortable as an insider, to see the world through one set of lenses and not notice what is happening around you. The pastor at First Mainline Church began to develop such a cultural awareness by digging into the history of the congregation and town. This awareness opened the pastor's eyes to the shifts (disruptions) that had taken place and were continuing to take place and impacting First Church. These changes included demographics but also much more. The pastor began to understand that both the church and the town had been through several "chapters" in their lives. He realized that the responses of both the town and the church to the realities of those times shaped the next chapters in good or not very good ways.

Second, insiders cannot be completely risk averse. The truth is that even those of us who play it safe are taking calculated risks daily. If you drive to work, then you are risking an accident. If you walk across a street, you are risking getting hit. One can look both ways when crossing the street and try to make sure nothing is coming, but there is no way to eliminate completely the risk of getting hit except to not cross the street. First Church had opportunities to take calculated risks, such as starting a second campus or a new worship service. The congregation decided not to cross the street. In part, it is because individuals like the current offerings. We often like what is being offered because we are uncertain about what may change. Innovation requires a willingness to risk.

Third, insiders need consistently to evaluate assumptions. We all make assumptions daily. Problems tend to arise when we are not regularly evaluating those assumptions—some of which may no longer be accurate.

It is not that the established churches were doing anything wrong, but as is so often the case, they were not revisiting their assumptions. Peter Drucker maintains that organizational problems are not the result of groups doing things poorly or even doing the wrong things. Organizations fail, he contends, because the assumptions on which they were built and on which they are being run no longer fit reality.[1] Could our congregations be taking for granted things that were safe assumptions in the past but no longer fit?

Those assumptions may include that our more established churches could not reach those being attracted by the new and different churches, that those new churches hold no appeal for "our" members, that people who attend our churches would obviously find the new churches lacking in a host of ways, and that the new expressions of church life are no threat to our continued growth and health. The established churches have failed to pay attention to the efficacy and long-term effects of many of these disruptions and have seemed to ignore additional constituencies that the new churches have been reaching. They continue to operate as if nothing has changed.

You can add to the list of flawed assumptions other notions that have steered once successful churches even after these assumptions no longer match reality. These include the following:

- There are lots of "young families with children."
- Most adults are married.

- Young adults will return to church when they get married and have children.
- Most people in our community already belong to a church even if they do not attend.

First Church assumed its current members would not find the growing congregations in the area attractive. When they started to dig deeper, they realized that some families left First Church because the youth and children's programs were more vibrant at the other congregations. Sound decisions depend on accurate information. Asking if the assumptions we are making (such as that members will not be interested in the new churches) are still valid or need to be reconsidered is crucial. Refusing to recognize the changing context and hoping things stay the same is not a worthwhile plan. Innovation requires relentlessly evaluating basic assumptions.

The most dangerous time for any organization is a time of success. At such times, we are unlikely to understand the reasons for our original success or the nature of our current vulnerabilities. We need to assess carefully and prayerfully our mission and how well we are achieving that purpose. In so doing, we may save ourselves from merely doing what we have always done in the past instead of doing those new things needed to further God's reign in our time.

Good and appropriate practices caused many churches to take hold and minister faithfully for generations, but many of those same practices may not be adequate for today. The test for any church is not found in the question, "Are we doing things our way?" Instead, the question should be, "Are the things we are doing bearing fruit?"

Chapter 6

Skills for Sustaining and Disrupting

Leading to both sustain and innovate requires at least three skills to achieve the goals most critical to the future vitality and faithfulness of your congregation:

- Practice outside-to-inside thinking. Here we learn how to plan from the perspective of those for whom the plans are intended.
- Use the so-that formula. This simple technique helps identify the outcomes most sought for any endeavor.
- Focus the agenda. Learning to limit the tasks attempted at one time can channel energy and time more productively.

SKILL 1: PRACTICE OUTSIDE-TO-INSIDE THINKING

Often churches and their leaders practice what might be called inside-to-outside thinking. They begin by focusing internally. That is, we want others to do what *we* assume to be valuable; therefore, we think that what is needed is to encourage others to participate in *our* idea. The beginning point is always *us* and what *we* offer. If you desire to enhance and expand ministry, a better approach could be called outside-to-inside thinking. This alternative begins from the perspective of those you are seeking to serve — those you hope to involve beyond the insider church leaders, those who are not a part of your church, those you most hope to reach.

Here is an example from outside the church world. Prescription medicine labels typically are designed with some things in large, bold print and others in smaller, lighter print. Usually, the most prominent feature on the label is the name of the pharmacy or other source of the medicine, along with location and contact information. In smaller text, one finds such things as dosage instructions and cautions regarding side effects. This is an example of inside-to-outside thinking. A pharmacy using this type of label is beginning with what they most want the user to see rather than with what is most important for the user to see. Today, some pharmacies reverse that logic by beginning with what is most important for the customer to see easily. Their labels give prominence to the dosage information most critical to the patient's health. Such a pharmacy does not begin with what they most want to say but with what the customer most needs to know.

Before planning anything, think about those for whom it is planned — those you want to reach. Then ask yourself,

- What are their questions?
- What are their concerns?
- What are their values?

Then you and those making plans will better be able to plan not only out of your own values and traditions but *also* in a way that is responsive to the needs of others.

Communication should also begin with those you hope to reach and their needs rather than beginning with what you are offering. If you want to see whether you and your congregation do more inside-to-outside thinking or more outside-to-inside thinking, listen to or read your church announcements. Do they begin with the person or group planning something or with those you most seek to reach?

HELP WITH SUSTAINING LEADERSHIP

We begin with a simple example to illustrate a focus on those you most want to reach. For over twenty years, the youth of your church have gone for a week each summer to poor communities in Appalachia, where they work with other youth. They have done repairs and other tasks that local agencies identify as most needed. Many of the youth see a world they never knew existed. It is a life-changing experience for some of them. However, in recent years, recruiting for the mission trip and raising the funds have become increasingly difficult. The connection between the experience of the youth and the ministry of the congregation seems more distant. As the pastor, you would like to see the youth group's effort linked more closely to the church's mission and to those in the congregation whose support is sought.

One of the many fundraisers the youth conduct for their trip is a car wash. You are asked by the adults who work with the youth to announce the car wash the Sunday before it occurs. They give you the wording for the announcement: "The youth of the church are sponsoring a car wash next Saturday from 10 to 2 in the parking lot. Money raised is for their summer mission trip. They hope everyone in the church will participate to help them."

Your first thought is "This will be easy." But then, as you reread the text, you notice it is written entirely from the perspective of "insiders." It's about the youth, their car wash, and money for their trip. None of it is from the perspective of the congregation to whom the announcement is directed. You decide to rewrite the announcement as your first step in strengthening a long-standing ministry but one needing improvement—a classic sustaining innovation. Here is the new announcement:

> Would you like to help poor communities in Appalachia this week? You can. For twenty years, our youth have spent a week each summer serving communities there. One way to join them in this service is to get your car washed next Saturday from 10 to 2 in the church parking lot. Cost is $X.00 per vehicle. If your car isn't dirty, you can make a gift in the offering, by mail, or online. If you want to help poor communities this week as part of your discipleship journey, the youth are providing you a fine opportunity.

HELP WITH INNOVATING LEADERSHIP

Your church has been growing. With that growth has come much change. Now it is clear to you and your congregational leaders that the next chapter for the church needs to focus on helping these new people explore their faith at a deeper level. The growth is exciting, but few opportunities are offered to challenge people to grow spiritually. You fear that if the congregation does not make this a priority, many people will be like the seeds sown along rocky ground in Matthew 13. They will spring up quickly, but because there is "no root," they will wither away.

The upcoming Lenten season provides an opportunity to emphasize spiritual growth and Christian discipleship. A task group develops a plan for three studies, each with six weekly sessions, from which participants may choose one. The task force report proposes an introduction to the courses:

Many churches offer special studies during the Lenten season. This year we will as well. We will offer three studies. The pastor will lead a Bible study. There will also be a study on one of the most talked-about religious books of the year and another study of the Holy Land taught by a member of our staff who has recently returned from there. I hope that all members will register for one of these studies.

Not the best approach. From where did these courses come? What interests or concerns among church members led to their selection? It all sounds like inside-to-outside thinking. You encourage the task group to keep working but from an outside-to-inside way of thinking. Instead of beginning by asking, "What should we do?" rather ask, "Whom do we most hope to reach?" This discussion produces a list including faithful members who attend everything offered, people new to the church in the past year (of which there are many), people who want to grow in their discipleship, and people seeking to renew their spirits and relationship to God during Lent. These groups are not mutually exclusive and will include overlapping constituents. However, each question addresses a primary factor that may lead people to participate in this program.

As you think about each of these groups, you wonder, What's on their minds? What's happening in their lives?

What has the past year been like for them? What questions are they asking? What topics come up in conversations? These questions lay the proper groundwork to select Lenten study offerings shaped by those you most hope to reach rather than by those who have something they wish to teach.

Here's the eventual newsletter message about the Lenten studies offered from this outside-to-inside planning process:

> The Lenten season is a time of spiritual assessment and renewal. We want to make sure you have resources to help you in this special season. This year, three studies will be offered.
>
> - Some of you have said you love your Sunday school class but sometimes want to go a bit deeper. You may be interested in the advanced Bible study class.
> - Others of you may shy away from Bible studies because you did not grow up studying the Bible. You may find the Bible 101 class just right for you.
> - And considering all the losses in our church and community over the past year, we are offering a class called "The Christian and Loss."
>
> If one of these studies is what you need to help you take your next faithful step with God this Lent, we would be honored for you to take advantage of that opportunity.

NOTICE THE DIFFERENCE

Notice the difference in these illustrations. Picture yourself hearing or reading these announcements. Does the change make a difference in how you will hear the announcement? Does the reframing make it more likely that you will hear it in a more positive way when it is presented in the revised version? Most people are far more open to opportunities when they can see some personal connection to the offering. These changes help define your congregation as sensitive to the concerns of those who look to their church for ways to grow spiritually.

In the case of the youth car wash, you don't want a newcomer mistakenly to hear about the car wash but miss its purpose. The car wash matters only as a way to fulfill your church's mission. Therefore, although a car wash enters the picture, you make it clear what's important—namely, that the youth of the church care about people who are poor or disadvantaged and that this concern is a part of the DNA of the congregation going back decades. If those learning of this opportunity share that concern, they have an opportunity to contribute. Even for those who do not participate at this time, you have sent a powerful signal of a key value of your congregation. Such examples build the culture of the congregation.

In the case of the Lenten study, under the original plan and language, you could easily have the impression that your church wants you to do something for them: attend the studies. Just as with the first car wash announcement, it appeared the church would like for you to do something for the church: help the youth raise money at the upcoming car wash.

Now think how differently you might hear or read the outside-to-inside versions. No longer are you being asked to do something for this congregation. The focus is on you and your circumstances. Instead of hearing, "We hope everyone will do this," you hear, "If this is something that reflects a

value or commitment you share, then we want you to know
it is offered for you."

SKILL 2: USE THE SO-THAT FORMULA

Even in the least effective congregations, much work is taking place. Pastors, staff, and congregants invest huge sums
of time and energy into a range of activities week after
week. This work can exact a significant toll—the frustration
that comes from being constantly busy without seeing many
results. The energy for future initiatives wanes as people
remember past elaborate plans that appear to have failed
to accomplish their goals. After all the planning and implementation, nothing seems appreciably different or, if it is
different, for the better.

The best leaders learn quickly that outcomes must shape
everything—that people must be clear about the purpose
of an endeavor—right from the beginning. Just as a farmer
must know the crop to be harvested before making any
efforts, so must we be just as clear about what change we are
seeking through any effort. We might tend to think that such
planning is important for new efforts but not for the ongoing ministries that have operated for years. Nothing could
be more wrong, however. That's why we offer this skill
to be used with both sustaining and innovating leadership.

One of the most important tools for both sustaining
and innovating leadership is the use of the phrase *so that*.[1]
These two simple words can transform well-intentioned hard
work into actual results that advance the mission. Here's
how to use the phrase:

*We will do X **so that** Y occurs.*

While this approach sounds simple, it is often harder than you think to articulate the "so that" of a given ministry. Even the most active church leaders often have difficulty articulating so-that statements for many common church activities, such as the following:

- We have a choir so that . . .
- We have ushers so that . . .

An example of one group using the so-that method to plan their annual vacation church school (VCS) is reported by Lovett and Tom Berlin in their book *Bearing Fruit.*[2] Here are some first attempts by the group of church leaders to clarify the "so that" of their VCS:

- Next summer our church will have vacation church school so that our children will experience vacation church school? [Really?]
- Next summer our church will have vacation church school so that children will experience church as fun? [Really? You won't need curriculum or teachers for that!]

The unspoken and assumed so-that often turns out to be that we do these things for the sake of doing them. Therefore, the most important question asked in all too many churches is not "Did vacation church school accomplish the purpose for which God led us to plan it?" but rather "Did we have vacation church school last summer?" The same is true for forming a choir, recruiting and training ushers, and preparing worship bulletins as well as virtually all ongoing activities. We too often do not ask about purpose but ask about activity. We are frequently so thankful that these things are happening that we do not question their fruits. In our minds, these activities were never intended to be ends in themselves.

HELP WITH SUSTAINING LEADERSHIP

Perhaps VCS is one of your ministries that needs improvement and new life. It occurs each year like clockwork, but you wonder if clarifying its purpose might be the best path to revitalization. Here's what one church did. After much careful and prayerful consideration, the church leaders developed their so-that purpose statement:

> Next summer our church will have
> vacation church school
>
> so that
>
> the children of our church will come to know
> and love God more
>
> and we will reach new children in the
> community with God's love.

Notice how a so-that statement changes everything. Without one, the goal is to have a VCS next summer just as we do every summer. You likely would begin planning with a series of tasks: setting a date, selecting the curriculum, recruiting teachers, recruiting other volunteers for refreshments and activities, and so forth. Then you would conduct the VCS.

But now imagine a different scenario. This time, the church has invested the time to discern the so-that statement. A so-that process depends on a congregation having named its mission, and your congregation has recently spent time deciding upon a mission statement. Leaders came together to name what it is they exist to do. They had listened, through the years, to others in the church and named what they understood to be their calling as a Christian congregation: "To make disciples of Jesus Christ and serve others." The mission may not be much different from that of some other churches, but it would now help them with the so-that process.

Given this mission, you developed a so-that statement for your VCS. Now everything you might have done before needs rethinking. For example, some of the people you would have invited to teach previously may no longer be the best choices given what this so-that statement would require them to do. And think about how other decisions may be altered based on this particular "so that." It may determine whether the VCS should be in the daytime or evening, whether a fee can be charged, what curriculum you will choose, who you must recruit as volunteers, where you will place the publicity, and whether the publicity will need to be in one or multiple languages.

In other words, the task is no longer to hold a VCS; it is now to ensure that "the children of our church come to know and love God more and to reach new children in the community with God's love." We can easily become so preoccupied with *what* we are doing that we lose sight of *why* we are doing it.

HELP WITH INNOVATING LEADERSHIP

Perhaps one of your church's priorities is to establish a ministry the church has never attempted before. It began when some younger, single members suggested that "our church needs a singles ministry." The pastor, having learned the benefit of the so-that formula, suggested that they talk with others and complete this sentence: "Our church will begin a singles ministry so that . . ." The ensuing give-and-take became a marvelous way to channel their interest in ways that fit the church's mission *and* the needs of singles.

Few groups can develop so-that statements well on their first try. There needs to be reflection, questioning, and feedback to clarify the desired result and ensure that it fits the church's mission. Lay, clergy, and staff responsible for a specific ministry need to be included. Participants in the ministry and those you wish to reach bring valuable perspectives. For those interested in a singles ministry, the first so-that statement was "Our church will begin a singles ministry so that singles in our church have a place to gather and share." Is the goal of a church singles ministry to provide adequate building space? Is real estate—a place—really the purpose? Such give-and-take causes people to take another step: "We want singles to have a place to gather and share *so that* . . ." This process can continue—using so-that questions until together, you identify the ultimate aim of the new ministry and how it grows out of and contributes to the mission of the church.

In this case, it served to convince the pastor and other church leaders of the importance of a church constituency to which little to no attention was paid. It also helped them understand how unready they were to begin a singles ministry. They needed to learn so much more and connect with many others before making even initial plans. Each step they take makes it far more likely that this innovation in their congregation will achieve its true purpose.

SKILL 3: FOCUS THE AGENDA

Whether practicing sustaining or innovative leadership, setting a few priorities is essential.

When Lovett was a seminary president, a new chair of the board of trustees took office. A long-serving trustee, the new chair was one of the most respected business, civic, and church leaders in the region. Not only the board but all seminary constituents had the utmost trust in his wisdom, commitment, and character. The new chair invited Lovett to join him for breakfast a few weeks later so they could talk about the president's one major goal for the coming year. When the day of the meeting came, Lovett was excited to report to the new chair because he brought not just one goal but thirteen! The chair of the board, just as kind and gracious as he was tough-minded, glanced at the list and said, "No leader can have thirteen priorities. Let's get together again in a month for you to report on your one major goal of the year."

How could the list be reduced? All thirteen were so important. Lovett employed a method he later came to use regularly to distinguish the big goals from among a multitude of good things. This process has to do with a series of questions to ask about everything on a list of goals to reveal where effort can make the most difference. Each question is answered with a numerical score between 1 (low) and 5 (high):

1. If achieved, how much difference would it make in the quality and strength of the organization or group one year from now?
2. If achieved, how much difference would it make in the quality and strength of the organization or group five years from now?

The first two questions put each project in a longer time frame. Some things that would be good to have or to do actually won't change the trajectory of the church.

3. How urgent is this project?
4. How vulnerable is the church if this project is not
   carried out?

These two questions take timing into account. Some projects would be helpful to do, but if the church does not
do them in the coming year, no harm will be done. The
church will be no worse for it. However, other issues are
such that without immediate attention, bad consequences
will come.

5. How much potential does this project have to
   make other things better?

New choir robes would be nice but probably would not
have a ripple effect across other ministries, whereas reduc-
ing the average age of participants is likely to reverberate
across virtually all aspects of the congregation.

6. How likely is success?

Success is never guaranteed, but its likelihood is one factor,
among others, that should weigh into decision-making.

7. How essential is individual leadership to the success of this project?

Some efforts require a leader's deep investment by virtue
of their position, knowledge, or skills while there are also
things that can just as easily be led by others. Reorganiz-
ing the children's educational program may be a dire need
but may not require the kind of attention from the pastor
that a new building program will require.

The steps in completing the table are to (1) list all the possible projects; (2) then in each column, give every project a numerical score from low to high, with 1 as the lowest score and 5 as the highest score; (3) total the scores for each project; and (4) sort them from highest to lowest score.

The scoring by itself does not determine priorities, but this exercise can provide clues to help you and others evaluate multiple options. Having as many people as possible complete this exercise is more likely to lead to creative conversations about priorities. The goal is not so much to eliminate options but to select those few efforts that are most critical to the church's mission and future. It is these priorities to which the congregation's clergy and lay leadership must devote their time.

PROJECTS	QUESTION 1	QUESTION 2	QUESTION 3	QUESTION 4	QUESTION 5	QUESTION 6	TOTALS
Sample Project	5	3	2	5	1	3	24

After Lovett made this first attempt at assessing priorities, he went to the next breakfast meeting with the board chair. He arrived with some worry because despite his new system and weeks of going over possible priorities, he still had not identified just one. He presented two to the board chair. Fearing he would be sent back to work on them more, Lovett was relieved when the chair said, "These two priorities are fine." Leaders need around them wise people who ask them the hardest questions and support them wholeheartedly. Lovett went on to serve eighteen years as president. When he left, in looking back over those years, it was clear to him and others who remarked on his tenure that these two early priorities had made the most difference.

This process does not cause leaders to work on nothing else but a few major goals, but these steps can identify those things needing significant attention. They also can create a lens through which to view virtually everything leaders do. Through that lens, leaders will be able to look more effectively at hiring, teaching, pastoral care, preaching, and many other aspects of pastoral leadership.

A few years ago, a group of pastors used the questions and process just described to sort out their goals for the coming year. After making long lists of hopes, challenges, opportunities, and projects facing them, they began scoring each potential priority. One pastor was totally surprised by how his rankings turned out. Coming into the session, he thought that building a new parsonage for his church was priority number one. He had a strong case to make. He served a church formed by the merger of two churches that chose to relocate, build a new church, and give it a new name. Building a new parsonage appeared to be a wise strategy, since the new church was growing along with the community's population, and the church owning a home for the pastor's residence fit their needs.

Given these circumstances, the need to build the planned parsonage was on the minds of many in the congregation as well as the pastor as they began the new year. There was agreement that the current housing arrangement was not working well for the church or pastor. If the pastor gave top billing to building the new parsonage, everyone would understand. However, as he did the priority-setting exercise, the new parsonage did not score nearly so high as some other possibilities the church faced. For example, the children and youth ministries had not previously been a priority because there were so few in those age groups in the two previous congregations. Now with the merger and the new location, it became clear to the pastor and other leaders that children and youth ministries would need to be a priority for the future.

What the pastor came to see was that the parsonage could be built without it being one of his or even the church's major goals. As needed as the parsonage was, when viewed against the church's mission and the desire to increase its vitality, children and youth ministries moved to a much more important place of significance. In fact, the more the pastor thought about it, if he and the church made too much of the new parsonage, members and especially guests might have the impression that he and the church were more concerned about building a house for the pastor than about focusing on an obvious need regarding children and youth that was at the heart of the church's mission.

HELP WITH SUSTAINING LEADERSHIP

This process identified the place of the parsonage project as important, but it was children and youth ministries that the pastor and congregation determined would be among the highest priorities for the future. Such priority setting is a good example of how a congregation can focus on what *leaders* may find to be primary leadership goals while, at the same time, attending to the range of important tasks that must be done to carry out and broaden ongoing ministry.

Sustaining leadership is about building upon the history and strengths of the congregation to advance the mission and move the congregation to an even more faithful and fruitful place in its journey to know and do God's will. Purchasing new choir robes, starting the worship service on time, and even building the new parsonage can still be done. Wise leaders learn how to use their time, influence, and resources for those central priorities.

Otherwise, leaders spend all their time on good things rather than on the "one thing [that] is necessary" (Luke 10:42 ESV), as Jesus said to Martha as she was fretting over so many things. Think of these "good" things as those commitments that are fulfilled in the same way as we turn the lights off when we leave a room. We do it, but the task does not occupy our best attention. A leader may remind a group that they are responsible for turning off the lights when the session is over. But does the group think it should take time in small groups discussing the best ways to turn off the lights? Of course not. But notice how many of our meeting agendas are filled with tasks that we should be doing as a matter of course, while we neglect to spend our primary energy on the few substantial matters.

Just think of all the routine things in your day-to-day life that you do. They might be returning a call, stopping by the store on your way home, helping a neighbor whose car won't start, renewing an insurance policy, and so forth. Even these and many other daily tasks do not shape your life. You can be counted on to do them, but they do not occupy the front of the mind. They will not overshadow everything else during the day. These necessary things do not make up the essence of your life, though you are glad to do them.

Leadership is not simply completing a series of tasks. It is helping people engage the pressing opportunities and challenges they face, and that requires careful assessment before setting those few priorities. You and your church can still do many fine things that do not rise to such importance. Focusing on those few crucial priorities, while continuing to do the necessary good things, can lead an already strong congregation toward improvements to shape a more vital and transformed church and community. And that is what sustaining leadership is all about.

HELP WITH INNOVATING LEADERSHIP

This same kind of focus on a few priorities, or perhaps only one, is crucial for providing effective leadership for those adaptive challenges in which the church is attempting something it does not yet know how to do, for which it has no positive recent track record, and for which the skills and resources are not in place. These efforts are not improvements on what you are doing but true innovation, at least for your congregation. If you are trying to "reach younger people" after over twenty years of average ages increasing among constituents, then doing what you already know how to do is not adequate. If you are trying to "reconnect with the community" when none of your church's current participants are from the immediate community, and no one in the church knows anyone in the immediate community, then naming a task group or approving a budget allocation means little. If you are trying to reach a racial or ethnic constituency when the church has never demonstrated that it can do so, then you are taking on a major challenge. What all these examples and others like them have in common is that the likelihood of success may be minimal under the best of circumstances; but if you are taking on such a vision and, at the same time, trying to accomplish other similar changes, failure for all the efforts is virtually assured. An organization, and perhaps especially a congregation, is unlikely to be able to accomplish more than one new and difficult challenge at a time.

Leaders routinely overreach when facing the struggles of a congregation. Instead of identifying the one innovative next step most critical for the church, the leader of the congregation may name and pursue a range of worthy innovations, with none of them receiving the required attention necessary for lasting change. Church leaders seem to think that if they are not pursuing all the possibilities they see, their aim is too low. Quite the contrary, it is in determining what one initiative is at the heart of a more viable future for the church's mission that true change occurs. If it is the right "new thing" a leader is pursuing, the efforts will yield far more fruit and a more varied harvest than anticipated. In this way, the one right thing, rather than the many good things, will become something of a field of energy out of which change will come well beyond your wildest imagination. Seeking to "reach younger people" may seem like a limited effort. However, if successful, the changes required to achieve the goal and the impact of the change on the congregation will go well beyond a change in age demographics. You will have a different church. Here, a singular focus on the right thing produces missional outcomes that are unanticipated and unexpected.

CONCLUSION

Leaders who continue doing the same things and hoping for different results will not be able to sustain or innovate well. The work of sustaining and innovating requires thinking differently about how we approach our work. Beginning with outside-to-inside thinking helps us move away from being so inwardly focused. The so-that exercise compels us to consider what we are doing and why we are doing it. As a leader, one can feel as if everything is important, but leaders must learn to focus attention on those things that will have the greatest impact over the long term. Continually practicing these skills will help any leader more effectively do the work of sustaining and innovating.

Chapter 7

Tools for Discerning
Your Next Faithful Steps

Dorie Clark claims, "The goal isn't to charge forward with
all ambitions. Instead, it's to nurture the right ones, jettison
the wrong ones, and avoid giving up too soon on viable
initiatives."[1] Clark's observation reminds us that in addition to caring for the basics and practicing good leadership to improve what they are already doing well, effective
leaders will undertake a few initiatives that go far beyond
improvements on what they already know how to do. Such
issues will enable a church to move into a new chapter in its
history. While continuity exists with the past, nothing in
it prepares leaders or their congregations to succeed in this
new endeavor. Selectivity is even more important for such
change efforts because the risks and potential downsides
are greater given the limited resources in most congregations. These challenges need solid grounding in a church's
mission and its context. They cannot be merely interesting
things another church has done or an individual's dream
that has not been tested by others. Even with the most careful discernment, risk is always present.

Innovation can be aimed at challenges or opportunities.
It may emerge from good or bad trends in the church and
community. Instead of thinking about how to take the next

step for an existing, well-functioning ministry, you are asking what God is calling your church to do in the near future
given your church's mission and context. It can range from
relocation to recommitment to the existing location. It can
involve new facilities or totally rethinking how your prop-
erty is used for ministry impact. It may primarily focus on
demographic categories such as age, race, or gender. It can
also involve an emerging mission to reach people with little
current interest in matters of faith.

Myriad good things may grow out of thinking about
what you and your congregation are called to do. But what
is it that God is calling your church to do in the near future?
In the previous chapter, we explained how Lovett had to
learn to focus on a limited agenda. He had to discern the
right goals for the moment given the context, mission, and
values of the organization. At that time, he developed a
series of questions to help him identify clues for the future.
What we are offering now is also a set of tools to help sort
through that myriad of good things and recognize what is
the next faithful step to which God is calling you and your
congregation.

As leaders, we sometimes are looking for something
new to just magically appear, but instead, imagine you are
looking into a kaleidoscope. There is nothing new within
the kaleidoscope as you adjust it. However, what you see
changes because you are looking at the same elements in
new ways. So it is that leaders learn to look at their contexts
from a range of perspectives, each providing its own set
of clues for the future. We offer these tools to help you do
such analysis and look anew through the kaleidoscope that
is your context.

With both sustaining and innovating priorities, these criteria for evaluating a way forward can be useful:

- Potential: What difference will it make?
- Reach: How will it help us reach new people?
- Readiness: Is the issue "ripe" enough to engage or can we "ripen" the issue?
- Fit: How will it align with our identity and values?

We share these criteria not as an exhaustive list but as a way of thinking about the work of moving a congregation forward to do sustaining and innovating ministry.

POTENTIAL

Evaluating the potential for a priority begins with two questions: What is possible? Will this option make a difference? A step toward these answers is to recognize the rhythms in your church.

All congregations develop rhythms. A part of a congregational rhythm may be following the liturgical year. A part of the rhythm is the fact that Mrs. Johnson parks in the same spot and sits in the same pew every week. A part of the rhythm is that breakfast is served after Sunday school on the first Sunday of the month. These familiar patterns in our faith practices may be invisible to us simply because we are not paying attention to them. This familiarity can also keep us from following God's calling. The issue is not that we do not have the potential to do something new; it is that we are comfortable with what we are doing. We need rhythm disrupters!

In chapter 1, we talked about Peter and Cornelius receiving visions from God. These visions were rhythm disrupters, causing both individuals to turn that kaleidoscope and to see their contexts in a new light. Although it would be quite beneficial if God intervened and disrupted our rhythms every time it is needed, we cannot count on that occurring. We have to find ways to create the disruption that will help us see, in the kaleidoscope, the possibilities God now has in mind for us. We can begin to examine what options have the potential for making the difference that will result from our next faithful step.

One way of disrupting a rhythm is to have someone who is not associated with your congregation visit worship and a few leadership meetings. Particularly for smaller congregations, this visitor does not need to be a trained consultant. It can be a trusted outsider such as a pastor, a member of another congregation, a professional skilled in observing groups, or perhaps a social worker or teacher—someone who has no personal stake in the congregation's future. This individual can share what they see and do not see while observing the various components of the church at work. For instance, the observer may note that the congregation says it loves families, but anytime a baby cries during worship, the parents get harsh stares from others in the pews. The observer may note that the congregation talks about being an inclusive community, but it is all white in a mixed neighborhood. The observer may not see activities for children in the pews or a crying room connected to the sanctuary that allows parents to still be a part of worship. The observer offers an honest assessment, sharing what they see and do not see.

Once the observer shares their perspective, the congregation can decide to alter the rhythm it has fallen into and seek a new way forward—an opening for thinking about what is possible, what has potential. In a congregation that talks about being an inclusive community, thinking about potential ways forward may mean connecting with their diverse neighbors.

In light of what they know about their neighbors (while still learning more), congregational leaders might start asking questions like "Will altering worship make a difference?" or "Will hosting community dinners make a difference?" The goal is to start thinking about what difference it will make to consider various ways forward. This reframing is possible only because the leader disrupted the normal congregational rhythm so that they could begin to see things differently and ask new questions.

We suggested that one way to create a disruption is to bring in an outsider, but someone internal to the congregation might also pay attention to its rhythms and be able to name them. If your congregation is connected to a denomination, they might be able to suggest possible observers. The key is to name rhythms that need disrupting and to consider potential ways forward.

REACH

As you search for the "right" priority, you will want to ask, "How will this help us reach new people?" It is one thing to think about whom we are seeking to reach, but it is another to discover what will help us reach them. And for that step, we must gather the information that will enable us to connect with someone new. Returning to our above example about families with babies, if this is an underserved population in our congregation, then reaching them as a family-friendly church is logical. The challenge is discovering what we need to know to ensure that we truly are a family-friendly church.

One place to start is by asking those in the congregation why they are connecting with you. You are looking for themes or commonalities that may emerge from their responses that can help you connect with others in the community. For example, you might learn that your congregation is one of only a few in the area with a family bathroom. While this may not have seemed significant to your leaders, it obviously is important to families. It is only through a conversation with those families with babies that this is likely to come to light.

A second important place to gather information that may result in surprising findings is directly from those who are underserved. If no one in the group you hope to serve is involved in the congregation, then you have identified that as a problem and will have to be creative and reach out to individuals in the community or try to learn from similar individuals attending other congregations. Here you might involve people from the congregation with broad and diverse networks within the community who could facilitate conversations with the group you are trying to reach.

Another helpful place to gather information is from census tools or the census itself. Many census tools (such as MissionInsite)[2] provide an overview of communities, including those who are attending faith communities, family breakdowns, and reported needs. This information is helpful because it allows you to better understand those you are seeking to reach in the community. You may learn that young families with children under five make up 20 percent of the community and that only 7 percent of those families are actively connected with a congregation. This means that trying to reach families is a wise move because they are an underserved population in your congregation, given the census data showing a higher percentage of families in this area. Sometimes you also learn something different from what you are hoping to hear, and this may mean having to adjust whom you are seeking to reach or where you are seeking to reach them.

A census instrument also often reports what groups need. For instance, it may report that the top three needs for families in a census tract are temporary daycare, reading enrichment, and beginner sports for young people. Given the resources of the congregation, hosting a parent's day out program one day a week—giving a break to a parent who is not working outside the home or who is working part-time—might be possible. Such a program could be a way of starting to connect with those in the community that you may not reach otherwise. A census tool can give you a lay of the land and help you think about possible ministry opportunities.

Communities are never static, so having an eye toward the future is important. Talking with city planners or other city officials, especially school leaders, about future plans for the community can be a helpful resource for congregations in considering the future. You may discover a plan to build a new elementary school and eventually a new high school in the community. This information supports your effort for reaching young families, but it also means thinking about teen ministry in the not-too-distant future. The mistake congregations often make is treating a current ministry that is going well as if nothing will ever change. The community is going to change, and thinking about it proactively and not reactively can help the congregation be more effective in reaching new individuals.

This criterion of *reach* for determining ministry priorities requires having the right information. It is good to have ideas regarding the new individuals you are seeking to reach, but if you do not gather the right information, then you may be setting yourself up for failure. Doing the legwork to understand the community can go a long way toward determining the focus for *reach*.

Remember that as you are exploring each of these criteria, you are enriching your understanding of the current context of your congregation. Then, as you look again into the kaleidoscope, a fresh image may emerge. That image may well help you focus on the next faithful step for your congregation.

READINESS

Naming what ministry has potential and determining how to strengthen the effort are significant steps. But a willingness to take the next faithful step toward something new is another. Many are not ready to consider doing something new that may alter the current course. Take again the example of the parishioners staring at the parents with crying babies. If worship attendance is still relatively strong, then members might not be ready to think about how they do and do not serve families. Some people might think there is no need to say anything and "upset the applecart." However disappointing the lack of interest is, the issue may become ripe only when attendance declines and keeping families is a high priority.

We must be discerning in congregations about when an issue is ripe. We do not want to address something before people are ready, and we do not want to do it after the opportunity has passed. Discerning the time when something is ripe means beginning with prayer. It is essential that no decisions are made by one person or one group. Praying as a community for guidance and listening for God to speak are crucial.

While prayer is occurring, leaders should have conversations with members of the congregation. These conversations are an opportunity for a dialogue between recognized leaders and others in the congregation to ascertain where people stand on a topic. Staying with the crying babies example, leaders may ask, "When we talk about being family friendly, what does that mean to you?" The leaders may discover a theme such as "We want a full Sunday school and children's church." This may mean that for some people, being "family friendly" does not include babies and children in worship. Follow-up questions and further conversation will be needed to see the range of assumptions about what "family friendly" means.

The congregational dialogues must include all members, especially those potentially impacted by any decisions. They may answer the question about what "family friendly" means by saying it means that grace is extended so all feel welcome during worship. Reading between the lines, an interviewer might conclude that some may not feel as if grace is currently being extended. Follow-up questions along those lines can tease out nuances. This information is invaluable and will help leaders hear all sides of the issue as they seek to discern readiness.

While still praying, leaders need to do what is often called a cost/benefit analysis. The phrase *cost/benefit* in this context may be misleading because the goal of a congregation is not to choose the path that costs the least in financial resources. Rather, leaders are seeking a way forward that stays true to their congregational values and leaders' and members' understanding of God's calling. Perhaps, for us, the term *risk/benefit analysis* might be more appropriate. We know that any change involves risk. Good contextual analysis can help us analyze if the risk is appropriate in this case and at this time. Continuing the example of the crying babies in worship, one way to approach this analysis is by considering the loss if all the families with babies leave. On the other side, what is the loss if those who seem upset by the crying babies leave because they are so uncomfortable with the commotion? The loss in either case can be numerical, financial, emotional, and spiritual. The cost of doing nothing may mean losing people from both groups, so this also must be considered. The benefit is that you have an opportunity to shape a congregational conversation around explicit and implicit congregational values and what those mean.

Leaders will have to figure out if prior steps are necessary to help the congregation prepare to talk about truly including everyone in worship. The first step may be a conversation on openness—a way for everyone to look at the reality that what *we* see and experience may not be what others see and experience. Many of us rely on personal experiences for interpreting the way things should be. My experience may be in worship where babies cry and are taken to another room, perhaps where a parent can listen to the service. I may feel that is how it should be. Others may have worshipped where babies stay, even when crying. Some may be unbothered. Another kind of "joyful noise," they say. But others experience it as a significant distraction. A conversation that unearths these assumptions can help foster a greater openness toward being more inclusive if our values regarding hospitality toward families are important. This is not an attempt to avoid the issue of what is meant by being family friendly, but it is a step toward discerning whether the congregation may be ready for *that* conversation. What is needed is to help the congregation take steps so all can participate in these crucial conversations in a positive way.

Readiness is a challenging criterion for evaluating priorities because the tendency is to move too quickly or too slowly toward change. Gathering the right information so you can make sure the issue is ripe requires actively listening and discerning. You may discover that you need to take preliminary steps before you can jump fully into more challenging conversations. Taking the time to determine readiness is key for sustaining or innovating.

FIT

Fit is about a congregation's identity and values; it is not a matter of a potential priority's familiarity. The criterion of fit often means disrupting a rhythm that is preventing you from fully living into God's calling. If your congregation claims to value families, but members stare at the parents when a baby cries, those coming with babies may not feel that the actions of the congregation and values are in alignment. In this case, finding a way to welcome babies into your midst would move you toward alignment with your values—creating an appropriate fit.

The story of Peter and Cornelius is helpful here. At first, gentiles seemed not to fit the faith community. How can those who are not circumcised fit among those who are? And yet, the actual values of the faith community—expressed in praying, worshipping, eating, and fellowshipping together—demanded the community include the gentiles. The challenge was helping those who perceived circumcision as the determining factor for fit to consider the actual values of the community. Circumcision was an important tradition, but the values of the community focused on loving God and neighbor.

We are assuming here that a congregation has worked to clarify its identity and values. If this is not the case, then it must begin with the hard work of naming identity and values before proceeding to consider fit. Being clear on your identity and values will help to shape your future and prevent you from making inappropriate decisions. For example, the identity of your congregation may be about primarily serving those who are retired. It likely is not a good fit to hire a youth minister if the plan is to continue a focus on serving the retirement community.

In this example, the fit is obvious, but the reality is that in our congregations, we deal with many more gray choices. What if you are thinking about whether to start trying to connect with those in nursing homes and retirement communities who may not be able to come to the church? In terms of values and identity, these people might fit who you are as a congregation. In terms of connecting with them, the fit is not as clear because other factors need to be considered—such as, How do we make the connection? At first glance this seems easy, but the congregation must consider whether it can provide transportation to bring people to it or whether the facilities will allow congregations on the premises if none of its members live in the community. Of course, the aforementioned challenges are not insurmountable, but it is important to think through all that is required and not just jump into a ministry. It is the challenge of discerning your way forward when the choice is not obvious that makes fit such an important issue.

There is no simple way to do this discerning process. Beginning with prayer as a community is always key, and continuing to pray during the discerning process is critical. Here are a few questions to help a congregation discern whether a sustaining or innovating effort is the right fit:

- Does the sustaining or innovating effort depart from our values and identity or simply stretch them?
- What do we have to offer?
- How can God work through us to make a difference in the lives of others?
- What resources do we have to do this work?

If your identity as a congregation is that you are a new church start with primarily twenty- and thirty-year-old participants, trying to pursue an innovation that focuses on nursing and retirement homes may depart from who you are. We are not suggesting such an innovation should immediately be rejected, but many questions need to be asked.

These are just a few of the questions you would need to consider. In chapter 8, we will discuss a model for innovation that will further explore the questions you need to consider. The point is to discern whether this direction will cause you to depart fundamentally from who you are and whether that is the direction you want to pursue. The innovation of including the gentiles in the fold, despite being a new community, did not cause the Jewish Christians to depart from who they were. They maintained their identity and values while being stretched on the issue of circumcision.

Consider whether the sustaining or innovating effort being considered is aimed at a short-term fix or has the potential for being a next faithful step. When numbers and finances start dwindling, we sometimes seek a quick fix. Suppose families who live in the community a few blocks away have children who go to a struggling school with a lower academic ranking. While we wait for new families to move into our higher-rated school zone, we halfheartedly reach out to those families a few blocks away as a stop-gap measure. This is a quick fix that may not be aimed at establishing an ongoing relationship. While the identity of the church may be that it is a community that focuses on families, it may not yet be open to considering all the families in the community for partnering and really want to connect only with those who are like it. The congregation would need to ask more questions about whether this form of outreach will fit their mission and values. Any effort that is a quick fix and is not moving toward building true and strong relational bonds is likely not a good fit. And yet, the congregation's mission and values might well be stretched to reach beyond their own school zone and perhaps enrich the makeup of the congregation—not only increase its numbers.

Fit is one of the very significant criteria we can consider in setting priorities for taking the next faithful step. Trying to be honest about how our efforts fit our identity and values is challenging because in any congregation, some people may have come to see their context and rhythms in a certain way. Turning the kaleidoscope to see things differently will help discern what options best *fit* with the identity and values of the church community. Attention to fit will be necessary for effective sustaining and innovating efforts of the leaders and the community.

CONCLUSION

The internal work to prepare for sustaining and innovating efforts is often overlooked. We who are leaders, along with a congregation, grow excited about doing the new thing and may fail to consider the steps needed to discover if the new thing is what is needed—that is, whether it is truly a faithful response to God's calling. Working with the criteria we propose—potential, reach, readiness, and fit—can help a congregation choose among myriad options to determine the next faithful step to which it is called. While there is always risk in doing the new thing, these criteria also help discern if this choice has the best chance to respond appropriately to where God is leading the congregation. The criteria are not to-do list items but gauges that help leaders assess the current context.

We constantly check gauges in our car to make sure everything is functioning correctly. We check our speed, we may glance at the temperature gauge to make sure we are not overheating, and periodically, we need to check for the change-oil light. These internal gauges make sure that the car is functioning in the way that it should. The criteria we have discussed in this chapter work in a similar way to ensure that as we consider sustaining and innovative efforts, we make decisions wisely. They give us a reading on where we are and what needs to be considered to move forward. Doing this work may not be as satisfying as the sustaining or innovative effort itself, but it can make the difference between whether the effort succeeds or fails. Constantly monitoring the internal gauges will allow us to see fresh possibilities as we make the necessary adjustments to take the next faithful step.

Chapter 8

A New Model for Leading Change

When leaders go into new situations, a common mistake they make is to think, "What I've done in the past was good enough to get me here; it will be good enough for the next step." Such is virtually never the case. That assumption is one of the prime causes of what some business leaders refer to as "derailment," when someone moves to a position of greater responsibility and things do not work out. In a similar manner, leaders come to think that because they are effective at making incremental changes through sustaining leadership, they can necessarily lead a congregation into new arenas to meet the changed context facing churches today.

Leadership is more than proficiently carrying out the practices that the role demands. Leadership requires guiding a congregation to take its next faithful step, which means engaging the big adaptive challenges it faces. You may be a skilled preacher, worship leader, pastoral care provider, and administrator. As important as those skills are, leadership finally is about more than *you*. Leadership is always about a group and not the leader. The ultimate test is not how well you perform but whether the people God has given you—as a people—are more faithful in their pilgrimage as a congregation.

Congregational leaders fall into the trap of thinking that approaches that have served them well for decades can guide them in a totally different situation today. Past methods of planning and implementing ministry may still work for ministries that are being done well. But old methods are often not helpful in addressing those things they are *not* doing or not doing very well.

A TRADITIONAL MODEL OF EFFECTIVE LEADERSHIP

Church leaders follow familiar patterns in their ministry. They are not written anywhere but rather carry the weight of conventional wisdom that seems to work. Sometimes the patterns do work, usually when a group is dealing with something they know how to do, something they have done for a while and do well. Let's examine this method using an example from one congregation that, for as long as anyone can remember, has had a food pantry that served a vast number of people in the community. One reason the ministry is so strong is that they follow an evaluative process each year to improve it.

After reviewing the year, they turn to brainstorming ideas to enhance the ministry and address some of the challenges that came to light during the review of the past year's work. Many ideas are suggested, and common themes emerge. From that discussion come the components of their plan. They know that success in implementing these changes requires making specific plans. They define their goals and objectives, identify the tasks required, assign responsibility for each task, and establish timelines for completion. They also know that everything cannot be done at once, so they need to prioritize tasks based on both their importance and the time of year by which changes need to be made. Using this traditional model, they develop a reasonable plan for the new year to improve the food pantry ministry.

Throughout the coming year, their plans unfold based on the projected timeline. They report to the church council, and the team leader for this ministry stays in touch with those responsible for each of the agreed-upon components of the plan. Month by month in team meetings, they celebrate the improvements made.

At the end of the year, they look back and can see the wisdom of the changes they made. They took a ministry that worked well and made it better. They will need to make more adjustments in the coming year to meet emerging needs, but for now, they take satisfaction in being able to say that the food pantry ministry is stronger today than it was a year ago.

That is a pattern repeated thousands of times every year in churches of every size and tradition. You know how to do it. Even when the implementation breaks down along the way, you still believe in the model because you have seen it work too many times to doubt its validity. However, you are so accustomed to this model for change that you are also likely to use it where it does not fit. The result is similar to using a tool not designed for the task at hand.

You have a method for improving ministry that works well with things you know how to do and do well. Your mistake would be concluding that the same model will work for those things you are not currently doing or not currently doing very well. Let's see why this process fails.

You believe you know how to develop a plan. You gather people with responsibility or interest in the subject at hand. For example, if your church has not had a functioning youth ministry in the past twenty years, you may decide to begin a youth ministry—a major innovation. You know it will require work and creativity. A few families in your church have teenage children, and many more youth attend a nearby high school and occasionally participate in the congregation's outreach and service activities. You have hopes that youth ministry, which meant so much to longtime members as they were growing up, can flourish again.

A task force is formed. Members are pleased to serve and bring both enthusiasm and ideas. As usual, the first step is brainstorming about how to improve the church's ministry to youth. As with improving the food pantry ministry, this group gathers the ideas into categories and selects those things that are most appealing. Items on the list include having the youth read Scripture in worship once a month, repainting the "youth room," hiring a part-time youth worker for the summer, and in the spring, recognizing those graduating from high school. There are many other parts of the plan, but these give you an indication of the kinds of things that emerged from their idea sharing.

As with the good work done with the food pantry improvements, a timeline is developed, and assignments are made. Monthly reports are given to the church council, and accountability is maintained so that each component is happening as planned throughout the year.

By the end of the year, the task force is frustrated. Each element of the plan took place as scheduled, but there is no apparent change in the congregation's connection with and impact on the youth of the church and community. If guests came to church and asked how their children could participate in the youth ministry, there still would be little to offer. You know the ideas were good. Some task force members saw them work when they were growing up in this church or in other churches they have attended. The reality is that you never had much of a chance that the plan would bear fruit. You are using a process designed for what you already know how to do and do well. The process is inadequate because it assumes more experience and relevant knowledge from church leaders than one can reasonably expect for a new initiative. Current leaders will bring much to the planning, but you have no recent experience doing youth ministry, much less doing it well. The sustaining process does not equip you for this endeavor when what you need is to practice innovation.

A MODEL FOR LEADING INNOVATION

Leadership for innovation will take you where you have not gone before, haven't gone recently, or haven't gone very successfully even when you have tried. Innovation cannot use the sustaining model of incremental improvement. The sustaining model works for something like the food pantry ministry because the purpose of the ministry is established and can be used to guide the planning, and the church has demonstrated it can carry out this ministry well, as evidenced by the fruit the ministry bears.

You are now undertaking something for which you possess the willingness but not the needed knowledge, experience, or capabilities to accomplish. Therefore, the beginning point must be different. You could begin with making plans to improve the food pantry ministry because years of groundwork have paved the way for the coming year's work. Also, participants knew the ministry well, had firsthand experience with it, and had done their homework by gathering feedback on the past year's performance. Now you have none of those resources to draw on for your new initiative.

Often, a lack of knowledge and resources does not stop us from proceeding as if we know what we are doing. If you knew everything needed to reestablish a vital youth ministry, you would have done it without waiting twenty years. But you move forward, suggesting ideas and plans as if you know far more than you actually do.

A NEW STARTING POINT

You cannot make plans until you determine the change you seek from your efforts. This is different from setting a goal of beginning a youth ministry. The change you seek is the impact you envision because of this new undertaking. How will life be different for the congregation and its members, as well as for the larger community, because of these efforts? Or, returning to the farming illustration, you must decide what crop you seek to harvest. No plans can be made apart from the change your congregation is seeking.

Here is the point at which the so-that tool is helpful. Continuing with the youth ministry effort, you need to complete the sentence, "We will develop a youth ministry so that . . ." Then you must think about how you want life to be different when the outcome is achieved. Remember, developing so-that statements can be hard. The first attempts usually are inadequate as a group reflects on whether this is really the ultimate outcome sought. This process requires patience, focus, and usually editing and reediting. You are not trying to capture every good hope you have for the youth ministry. You are trying to state the result, what is different from the current situation. The temptation is to use language such as "so that youth . . . know you care, have a place to gather, will experience the church as hospitable," and so forth. While ensuring that youth know that you care or providing physical space in which they can meet are good things, they are hardly distinctive callings of the church. Why do we want youth to know we care? What difference might that make in their lives? What do we hope will result from providing space for youth? Another way of thinking about the result is to ask, "If this initiative works, what will be different one year from now?" This can steer you away from focusing only on feelings and intentions. Even the most spiritual of efforts lead to observable changes, so you need to ask, "What would those be?"

What change would tell you that the youth ministry you envision is making a difference in the lives of the youth, their friends and families, and your church? Without such a target, you have no basis for any plans. Here is a statement one church developed after many attempts that never seemed to capture a result that could adequately guide them: "We will do all our ministry in such a way so that increasing numbers of youth worship, study, serve, and build relationships that support their growth as disciples of Jesus Christ."

There are some advantages to this statement compared to some of those mentioned earlier. It puts the focus not so much on what you hope youth will do for us (attend our services, participate in our committees, and the like) but rather on what *we must do* that is inviting for youth and that leads to their growth as disciples of Jesus Christ. It also leaves open what it means to "do all our ministry in such a way." It could lead to rethinking how the church does virtually everything, including its worship, ministries, and governance. Rarely do the decisions in those arenas take account of the interests and growth of the youth. On the other hand, this so-that statement makes possible distinctive youth-specific ministries. Whatever your purpose statement is, it will guide every decision to come.

LEARNING

Many leaders are familiar with Ronald Heifetz's distinction between technical and adaptive challenges. Technical challenges present a clear problem that has a clear solution for which you already have the necessary authority and resources. On the other hand, an adaptive challenge is one in which either the problem's definition is unclear, the solution is unclear, or the authority and resources needed are uncertain. The most important tasks for leaders, once they determine that an issue is indeed an adaptive challenge, are for them to learn themselves and to guide a learning community.[1] Acknowledging their limited knowledge and experience is essential to avoiding yet another failed attempt to do something they have never done well or have not done for a long time.

Once you know that reaching the desired outcome involves an adaptive challenge, you are ready for the most important task of innovative leadership: *learning*. The question is, "Given this desired outcome, what do we need to learn?" Assuming your desired outcome involves a major change, you will likely need to learn a great deal, and as you learn, you will discover just how much you still do not know. You are attempting something for which you have no significant experience doing well. That fact requires a stance of deep humility for all involved. The temptation is to jump ahead into planning and action, but you are not close to being ready for that.

Beginning all talk of this new initiative with "What do we need to know?" and "What do we *still* need to know?" assumes a learning phase out of which, in due time, may come plans. A good so-that outcome brings with it a learning agenda essential to fruitfulness. As you saw with the hospitality ministry example, the beginning point of learning is the current state of any relevant ministries that may be assets or perhaps liabilities as you move forward. If this assessment part of the learning process is done well, then insights and clues for the next steps may emerge quickly. Simply giving attention to a subject through analysis and conversations usually surfaces insights on which the new effort can build. For example, a church wanted to engage the entire membership more fully in volunteer service in the community. They began by inquiring about those already serving in the community and the nature of their service. Leaders discovered far more volunteer activity beyond their congregation than they had anticipated, identifying important members with a heart for such service. They thereby discovered a much broader range of opportunities for volunteer service than they had previously imagined.

The learning agenda must go far beyond exploring the current state of things in your congregation relative to the initiative. These questions may help you expand your conversation partners:

- With whom do you need to talk?
- Whose engagement is essential for this effort to thrive?
- Where do you need to visit?
- Who has experience in what you are attempting?
- Who works closely with the constituents for which this ministry is intended?
- Who should know you are beginning this effort?
- With whom might you partner?
- What internal and external information relevant to the initiative do you need to gather?
- What do you need to read?
- Who are the most trusted sources on this issue?

Establishing a learning culture is essential. The information gathered must be shared with all involved in the planning process. There may be ways to share some emerging ideas with other church leaders and perhaps the congregation. Keeping everyone connected to the endeavor and its purpose will help with congregational acceptance later. You are building a common foundation of insights and information on which future decisions will depend. Many members of the team need to participate in the research, study, conversations, and field trips required. Conversations in which team members tell what they are learning for the benefit of others will generate questions and common findings worth noting. You also need to share the most pertinent elements of what you are learning with your congregation's governing body and perhaps the congregation. This can often be done effectively by reporting from the team on what we are learning. What can follow is an invitation to those beyond the planning team to offer their insights and perhaps recommend others with whom the team might be talking.

As you explore both the successes and failures of various congregations, avoid the temptation to copy another church's effective ministry. Assess all you learn considering the different circumstances of your congregation and community so you can use ideas in appropriate ways. Ask everyone with whom you talk, "Who else should we contact?" Always ask what sources have been most and least helpful to them. Learn from them all.

Perhaps most important, this learning must go deeper than the mind. It requires a deep immersion in the topic, constituents, other congregations, and community. The more you get to know others and understand their experiences, the more all will learn. People normally are not moved to do something entirely new based strictly on logical arguments and facts. For example, a pastor in a rural area discovered that there was not a church in the county that offered a contemporary worship service. That absence meant little to the members, since they were happy with their traditional worship and not prime candidates for a contemporary service. However, the pastor knew there was a high school in the county and that there were many younger people for whom a contemporary service might be inviting.

Instead of bringing a proposal to begin a contemporary service to her members, she began by asking a few at a time to join her in attending contemporary services on Saturday evening or Sunday evening at churches within easy driving distance. She was asking for partners from among her church members to help her learn more about the pros and cons of contemporary services. The members were happy to help, though they were unfamiliar with contemporary services and thus a bit anxious about what they would experience. Every few weeks, however, some of them would accompany the pastor to these services and then talk about what they experienced. Then after several of these visits, all who participated came together to debrief.

As it turned out, everyone learned a great deal—and not what they expected to learn. For one thing, they discovered that there is no such thing as "contemporary worship," if by that you mean a service that looks the same from church to church. They easily identified common elements but were more struck by how each church had shaped its worship to fit its context and constituents. It was freeing for them to know that services could be contemporary without having to copy another church's service. They also discovered a broad range of practices related to space, music, preaching, and participation.

This learning by engagement led to an openness to contemporary worship that none expected to have. While there was a willingness to begin a service in their building, they realized that the location and layout of their church would not be conducive to a contemporary service and those they most hoped to reach. Instead, they made a significant financial commitment to rent a site familiar to youth. They also modified their traditional worship time to make possible their pastor's involvement in the new service. This congregation's learning through experience illustrates how a group was able to make more informed and faithful decisions through their visits and conversations—and not simply from someone reciting facts to them.

The goal of your learning is to understand the current situation and gather insights for the future. You cannot learn all you need to know, but you can uncover some assumptions and come to some givens that will serve you well as you get started. You are not trying to construct a comprehensive plan but rather establish a platform from which you will learn more. Always remember that while others will know more than you about the subject of your innovation, you and your team are the experts on your congregational history, culture, and values. You are always looking for connections beyond the two types of knowledge—facts and experience—on which you can build.

FIRST STEPS

Now you are ready for planning—but not the kind with which you are most familiar through sustaining leadership practices. In all likelihood, this will not be a plan for as long as a year, though it could be. Time frames are likely to be weeks and months when you are testing options and assumptions. It certainly will not be a plan for which assignments are given, and accountability comes by merely assuring that people have done what they agreed to do. Of course, the tasks must be done, but the goal is learning.

You are developing tentative plans from which you can learn and that you can adjust. The question at every step along the way is not "Did we do what we planned?" but rather "What did we learn, and what does it mean for our next steps?" For example, you may discover quickly the unspoken assumption that your youth ministry initiative would involve only one group of "youth." You learn that age differences matter so much that to ignore them is foolish. Now weeks into your efforts, wholesale changes need to be made in your tentative plans. This is not a problem, since your goal was never to implement your plans for the long term but rather to achieve your ultimate outcome, which requires such learning over and over.

The line between beginning efforts and accomplished outcome is never straight. It is far more circular, and you experiment, learn, build on success, and revise when things do not work. In the meantime, not only are you learning, but you are building a learning culture among everyone involved who is committed to achieving your outcome. The learning community is growing, and the band of those who understand the effort and invest in it is broader.

INNOVATING IN PRACTICE: A RECAP

Practicing innovative leadership is a necessity for all who care deeply about the faithful and fruitful stewardship of your congregation's mission. Maintaining "what is" never is sufficient; and the more the church, community, and society are changing, the more attuned leaders must be to those changes and their implications for the church. Matt Miofsky and Jason Byassee capture the challenge well when they say, "In our churches, we often overestimate the cost of trying something new and underestimate the cost of doing nothing."[2]

RECALLING YOUR THREE LEADERSHIP IMPERATIVES

Your attention must be focused on three things as you plan your own priorities and work with congregational leaders and staff to set congregational priorities:

- the basics on which all else depends
- the sustaining efforts most critical to the organization's ongoing mission and fruitfulness
- the innovation efforts most critical for the church's next faithful step

CHOOSING KEY CHANGE PRIORITIES

In the previous chapter, we said that in addition to caring for the basics and practicing good management to improve what you are already doing well, vital congregations identify a few initiatives that can take your church into a new chapter in its history. We suggested that these criteria are useful in identifying those priorities:

- Potential: What difference will it make?
- Fit: How will it align with our identity and values?
- Reach: How will it help us reach unserved or underserved people?
- Readiness: Is the issue "ripe" enough to engage or can we "ripen" the issue?

Think of looking into a kaleidoscope. Each of the four criteria represents a different turn of the eyepiece. The elements inside the kaleidoscope stay the same, but you see a new image with each turn. Each criterion gives you a chance to see fresh possibilities. Once the priority is determined, you are ready for the next steps.

DETERMINING WHAT GOD IS CALLING YOU TO DO

Leadership for something you are not currently doing or not doing well is different from making incremental management improvements—changes you identify through your experience. Efforts you are not doing or not doing well require new construction, not renovation. You first must decide what change you believe God is calling the congregation to make. Farmers do not know what to do until they decide what crops they hope to harvest. Builders cannot begin until the nature of the structure is determined. So it is with the most spiritual of ministry endeavors. You must determine what fruit you hope God will provide from the harvest of your efforts.

EXPLORING WHAT YOU NEED TO LEARN

Next is learning—and resisting the temptation to begin doing things. You don't know enough to do things yet. Remember, Heifetz says an "adaptive challenge" is one that requires you to learn before you can act.

TAKING INITIAL STEPS

As you learn, you will continue to confirm or revise your ultimate outcome, even as you begin to think of initial steps that will help you test out the assumptions behind your thinking as well as other critical aspects of the effort. Many of the learning activities discussed previously will take place at this time. The innovation chart refers to this phase as "initial plans and first steps." While you are "doing things," the primary task continues to be learning.

EVALUATE, LEARN, AND TAKE NEXT STEPS

Each of the initial steps leads to evaluation, learning, and subsequent next steps based on what you have discovered. With each step, you are growing wiser and more focused on what you still need to learn. Some of your ideas may fall away as a result of your testing, but others will arise. Those working as a team should gain energy and confidence from their growing knowledge and experience.

THE NEED FOR NEW KNOWLEDGE AND SKILLS

The decline of participation in mainline and other congregations is not news. Mainline denominations have been working to reverse negative trends for years. We believe change requires a new way of thinking. The knowledge and skills a pastor needed in past decades are not irrelevant, but now they have to expand. The new competency requires sustaining and innovating leadership practiced well and at the same time.

Wise leaders consider how much time and effort they put into sustaining leadership—building on the strengths of the congregation and minimizing its weaknesses. They also recognize that they cannot rely on sustaining leadership alone to help God's people take the next faithful step given new and ever-changing cultural and social contexts. They also need to practice innovative leadership. This both/and approach requires new knowledge and new skills.

Chapter 9

Innovating in Practice

In this chapter, we explore steps in the life of a congregation we call Broadway Church, in which innovative leadership is required. That means the goal is something that the church is not already doing or is not doing well. Mere improvement is not enough to address the problem. The church's mission can be served only by rethinking basic assumptions and making changes.

REACHING YOUNGER PEOPLE

Broadway Church needs to reverse decades of a trend that is out of alignment with the church's mission. The discernment process went in many directions before a consensus emerged around the goal of reaching younger people. The average age of the congregation had consistently increased for a generation. The percentage of participants aged seventy and above increased each year, with a growing percentage of financial support coming from this same group. Many educational and mission ministries died from a lack of younger energy and participation. On the positive side, reaching younger people became a direction that, if fruitful, could revitalize a host of dimensions in its congregational life. This goal grows out of the church's greatest vulnerability (aging) and its greatest opportunity (a surrounding younger population). The goal expressed as a so-that statement was simple: "We will do our ministry so that our congregation serves an increasingly younger constituency of growing and serving disciples."

GOALS ARE FILLED WITH ASSUMPTIONS

This goal, like so many, seems straightforward. But goals are loaded with assumptions. Imagine that you are the pastoral leader of Broadway Church. Along with other church leaders, you will need to identify those assumptions so they can be tested. Fortunately, the process of goal setting produced information that helped confirm some of the assumptions. For example, the goal assumes that the congregation is, in fact, getting older, which is documented. It also assumes that the surrounding population includes persons younger than those the congregation is now reaching. This was confirmed as well.

Some other assumptions include the following:

- The goal is tied to the church's mission, "to make disciples, grow disciples, and send disciples." However, you do not know how well these factors matter to those outside the church or whether one might have more appeal as an entrance point for new and younger people.
- You assume your church desires younger members and think they are unaware of some of the implications of the goal.

LEARNING COMES NEXT

You begin with obvious assumptions but need to identify further what learning is needed to accomplish the tasks required for the goal. This learning agenda may include the following:

- Data. Before deciding upon the goal, you gathered helpful information, but what else can you discover about both the church's and community's demographics, particularly related to age?
- History. What characterized the congregation's earlier chapters? Who knows the stories? What does today's context have in common with earlier periods? What differences are significant?
- Forecasts. Who in the community works with forecasts and projections? The schools plan ahead. There may be an economic development group. What can you learn from the most recent census figures and other sources about community trends?
- Best practices. What churches have done well in reaching young or younger people? Who can visit and meet with their leaders? What clues and commonalities do you discover?
- Additional research. What topics should you explore given the nature of your goal?
- Community relationships. Who and what organizations in the community know more about and have more experience with engaging younger persons? What have they learned? What trends do they see? What is working or not working for them?

The goal of learning is not only to collect information. The goal is to gather insights that generate conversations among your team and then with others. "The key to dealing with complexity is to focus on having good conversations" is the way two writers on innovation put it. "A good learning conversation is qualitative. It is about assumptions, not numbers."[1] Such learning helps shape your orientation toward the goal. This learning will expand your horizons in some cases, but in others, it will narrow your focus. You come to realize that approaches that once worked, or that you thought might work in the future, no longer seem viable.

The steady process of gathering information, sharing information, and then discussing that information in light of your goal builds a group of people who are increasingly adept at assessing what all of you need to know to move forward. As you make progress, you will slowly coalesce around a few basic understandings about your context, your goal, and what may be needed to take the next steps toward that goal. These insights become the foundation of your planning. On some topics, you will move from speculation to certainty. Some guesses will be confirmed or disproved.

FIRST STEPS

The first steps you take are actually a continuation of the learning process. You are not ready to lay out a grand plan with timelines and assignments. But you do need to move from learning from others to learning from your own actions and experiments. Through your learning up to this point, especially the conversations you have had with one another, you have a much better assessment of both your goal and the possible means to accomplish it. This may be a time to make sure the goal is still appropriate as originally worded. From the beginning, you have been on a journey from hunches and hopes to knowledge and insights. The ability to adjust based on new information is critical.

Next, you need to find the most efficient and least expensive ways to test some of the current assumptions that undergird your goal. Some of this will feel like an extension of your prior learning. At the beginning, you had the most basic of assumptions, without which you would not have set your current goal. But now you realize you need to move beyond simply the data that led you to the goal, and you discover you are working with additional assumptions that need to be tested. For example, you may conduct focus groups with those central to your goal—those you hope to reach, key leaders crucial to this goal, and partners who would be needed. These conversations will enable you to test whether reaching younger people is indeed a realistic goal for Broadway Church and will also help you make new connections and build relationships. You may also plan one-time events that give you a chance to test the waters around interest, networks, and communication methods. These initial activities permit you to identify potential new partners who, in a sense, "raise their hands" by showing special energy and interest. These persons are valuable in testing out some of your planned next steps and linking you to others.

LINKING WITH THE LIFE OF THE CONGREGATION

Obviously, there needs to be a leadership team for any major endeavor. By now, you have such a team, and you want to avoid the mistake that many churches make as they take on something new. Such churches identify a group of people, establish them as a task group, perhaps give them a budget, and encourage them to accomplish the desired goal as the rest of the church continues as is. This is a formula for disaster. It never works. The best task groups or teams need access to the breadth of the congregation's leadership, ministries, and resources. A worthwhile innovation must engage a church throughout the life of the congregation.

Here is one way to think about such a strategy. What if you thought about your goal as a vision that, for the near future, will function as the church's "invisible leader"? You would then ask the leaders of every ministry and work area of the congregation to think of their plans for the coming year through the lens of reaching younger people. The question you ask each group to answer is, "How do we plan our work in the next year so that we are serving a somewhat younger constituency a year from now than we are today?"

The leaders will need education to buy in to this strategy. Expect some resistance. Many see their focus as unrelated to the age of those with whom they are working. However, in practice, amazing new possibilities will arise from unexpected places. Here are examples from one church seeking to reach younger people:

Trustees (originally resistant; "We do bricks and mortar")
- Renovated the nursery and preschool-age facilities. Most trustees had not been in that space in twenty years. One remarked, "I wouldn't let my grandchild come here. It's too dangerous."

Music ministry staff and choirs (originally resistant; "We thought we were about music")

- Organized a children's choir, an idea they had discussed for years.

Missions committee

- Organized a youth component to their already established Volunteers in Mission program.

Children's ministry staff and teachers

- Having combined classes across a wide age range due to the difficulty of securing teachers, the education program leaders reorganized these classes with more appropriate age groupings and more training for teachers.

Worship committee

- Younger and more diverse persons were invited to serve as worship leaders and ushers.
- Focus groups helped identify those aspects of worship most confusing to younger and first-time worshippers. The worship committee and pastoral staff could then change portions of the service or provide explanatory notes to make worship more welcoming to newer and/ or younger people.

Now that you are inviting your ongoing ministries to plan their work so as to involve a younger constituency, you will be taking steps toward your goal in multiple ways. This planning will alert far more people to the church's goal and help them see their ministries through its lens. Perhaps more significant is that any one of the ministries may accomplish *some* good by itself. But what each group is doing can come together into a synergy out of which amazing changes can come; thus, the groups make genuine contributions to the overall goal. What any one group does may do some good, but by itself, it probably cannot do much. For example, renovating the nursery area alone will make little change. However, if this renovation is going on at the same time as many other initiatives, the synergy of all the efforts can produce much significant change.

STEPPING INTO NEW WATERS

You have given attention to the efforts of your existing ministries to make changes that lay a foundation for your new goal. At the same time, you can see the reasons why a challenge requiring innovative leadership cannot be accomplished with incremental changes alone. While more modest changes are taking place, you need to explore the "new thing" you hope God will do in your congregation, taking you well beyond your current capabilities. You cannot enter a new chapter while only revising the current chapter. If you are to truly take the next faithful step that you have discerned God has for your congregation, you will need to identify new themes and new leaders—those that will lead to new accomplishments. You will need to step into new waters.

You have discerned and confirmed your goal, learned a great deal about the opportunities and challenges it offers, and engaged congregational leaders as partners in this adventure. Following all this initial work, what do you do next? By now, you should have some sense of a theory of change[2] or, as we will refer to it, a mission model that suits your situation.

You have a goal, but there are multiple ways to accomplish the goal. Some fit your context and capabilities better than others. For example, two environmental groups may have similar goals but different mission models. One may focus on influencing public policy and legislation. The other may purchase land to protect it from development. In each case, the organization is stronger and more effective when it adheres to its focus rather than trying to do everything.

The mission model for the Lewis Center for Church Leadership of Wesley Theological Seminary is to discern and share "strategic actionable insights."[3] The goal for the center is captured in this so-that statement: "The Lewis Center for Church Leadership is a trusted resource for church leadership ideas, research, resources, and training so that there is an increase in congregational and denominational service, vitality, and growth."

The goal of "an increase in congregational and denominational service, vitality, and growth" could be undertaken through various means. The Lewis Center concluded that it could best accomplish this goal through discerning and sharing "strategic actionable insights." Therefore, whatever the topic undertaken—congregational mission funding, community engagement, pastoral transitions, diversity, congregational visioning, or others—the beginning point is to draw from the research of others as well as our own to develop those strategic actionable insights that someone with motivation around the topic can use to move forward with confidence. Various means are used to share these insights—conferences, online learning, print and video resources, books, reports, workshops, and others—but the focus is always the same: sharing strategic actionable insights and continuing to learn more ourselves.

Let's look at some options for your entry point to achieving your goal. The one you choose will need to be the right one to fit your situation. You cannot begin by trying to do everything.

CHILDREN

As sad as you are about not having a critical mass of youth in the church for many years, you realize that a fruitful entry point to achieving the goal of serving a younger constituency is children. Members do not have large numbers of children, but there are groups of children who are close enough in age to one another that classes and activities would make sense. The parents of these children are relatively new to the congregation. Some of them are already uneasy about there being so little ministry for children, but you have superb facilities for children's ministry that would require primarily refreshing, not renovation. Your mission model becomes to build a younger constituency from the ground up. If you focus on this cohort of younger children, the stage is set to serve many more children of this age, and most importantly, you lay a foundation on which you can build your overall children's, youth, and young adult ministries one step at a time as these children get older.

YOUTH

You may decide that a mission model centered on youth is the logical approach for your congregation. Focusing on youth is usually difficult if you do not have a solid foundation on which to build. But you may decide that you have enough youth and connections beyond the congregation that give you a good chance of success. You believe your facilities and staff are sufficient for focusing on youth.

MISSION

Another model might be using service and mission efforts as the entry point for involvement by more and younger people in the community. One church that used this approach began with a Great Day of Serving, in which members helped people in their community beyond their own membership. That led to a Great Week of Serving. Then they invited other churches in the community to participate. Eventually, the effort became a community-wide Great Week of Serving. Their initiative to establish the innovative, multiyear effort became their identity in the community. Where before their church had been one of many that were viewed comparably, now they had a distinctive identity in the minds of the community. They were the "serving" church. They accomplished much good and grew younger and more vital as a congregation at the same time.

NEWLY RETIRED

As counterintuitive as it may sound, focusing on newly retired people could actually lead to reaching younger people. This could actually lead to one dimension of the focus on reaching younger people. This initiative developed at a church in a locale popular with the newly retired. While the congregation was primarily composed of people ages seventy and older, leaders discovered that many of the people moving to their area were in their fifties and sixties. Some were partially retired. All were active. The congregation realized that even with fewer children and youth in the community, they could put their focus on a younger segment of their community that, up until then, the church had not considered a priority.

REENGAGING THE COMMUNITY

You may discover, through exploring mission models such as those just discussed, that there is a more basic need in your community, perhaps one your congregation is better positioned to address. For example, the above models all point to one reason these church leaders believed that reaching younger people was the congregation's innovative need: its growing disconnection from the community. Perhaps you are learning, through these steps, that the church becomes younger on its way to becoming more integrated into the community and thus more effectively serving the needs of the community. As you look back at your current mission statement, which includes *sending* disciples, you may see that sending implies "serving the needs of the community." In fact, you may decide to go back to your mission statement to make that component more explicit.

CONTINUE TO TEST ASSUMPTIONS AND MONITOR PROGRESS

One of the reasons for such careful discernment and planning in the early stages of any innovative effort is that the tendency in many organizations, including churches, is to let the allure of an ambitious goal hide just how ill-equipped the organization is to do new things. Leaders may be tempted to focus on the new initiative, as if merely naming it will make it come to pass. There is power in ideas but not enough to take the place of careful implementation. Change initiatives in churches invariably fail not because the ideas are poor but because the implementation is inadequate. Unfortunately, some leaders think that implementation is a stage in which they can step back, much as they would when assignments are made for a sustaining improvement. But the rigor of the planning process must now be matched by the care with which implementation proceeds.

Remember that innovative leadership is about those things you are not doing or not doing well. While careful accountability for implementation is essential, just "getting the task done" is not the ultimate goal. You must continue to nurture a learning mindset—to evaluate whether you are making progress, to learn, and to improvise throughout the process. Set markers and test them against reality. You may discover clues for continuing as planned, reconsidering your direction, or naming problematic issues that must be examined. While perseverance will be necessary, you will need people who can help you make some objective analysis of how things are going. Stay in conversations with constituents and with wise people in the congregation and community. Talk with those whom you trust to have a good understanding of the "why" of your goal, the steps you have taken, and if the progress shows you are moving in the right direction.

If the result were certain, the undertaking would not be innovative. Established churches are adept at sustaining themselves, which is why they have come to be established. They are challenged by a need for originality. What you are doing with an innovation project is asking a portion of the congregation to function as the whole congregation had to in the church's earliest days. Few things were certain because there was no tradition. Matters of worship times, music, education, small groups, facilities, and finances all had a tentative nature as appropriate patterns and practices were discovered. The mission of the church did not change, but how that mission was implemented continued to evolve over the early months and years. Now again, you are asking Broadway Church to think and plan and dream as they first did.

INNOVATING IN PRACTICE

There are many books on innovation and models for achieving it. It is our hope that we are offering a way of organizing your approach to innovation. No matter what model you choose, organizing your work in the way we suggest should help you discover the focus of your next faithful step and increase the likelihood of success. To that end, we recap the central characteristics for organizing your work on innovating:

- Develop a clear so-that statement that delineates where you are seeking to go.
- Be honest about the assumptions you are making as a congregation. (This may require the assistance of someone who is not beholden to the worldview of the congregation.)
- Be diligent in learning all that you can from as many resources as possible.
- Create a lens through which the entire congregation can view their various roles and contribute to the new innovation effort.
- Develop and test appropriate mission models.
- Continue learning, evaluating, and adapting the models as you move forward.

These organizing characteristics will help you innovate in a manner that is not dependent upon congregational size, financial assets, or the strength and experience of church leadership. The starting point for every congregation is different, and this difference is captured in the so-that statement that will be realistic for your context. The attention should be on developing a statement that focuses on something you are not doing or not doing well. A particular innovation will be unique to each congregation, and the innovating process is something that every congregation can practice.

These organizing characteristics also remind us that innovating is ongoing work. It is easy to believe mistakenly that once we do something new, our work is done. Many congregations are struggling today because of that mindset. They started off with a strong missional focus of reaching their community, had some success, and felt they could stop and celebrate their success. Innovating, as we have seen, is setting out to do something you are not doing now or not doing well, in contrast to sustaining a practice or ministry that you discern should be continued and strengthened. You should not reach a point as a congregation where you stop considering your next faithful innovation.

The energy and time required for innovation can cause some leaders to lessen their attention to sustaining leadership. But innovation requires that leaders help the whole people of faith take their next faithful step. This requires a sensitivity to those who are central to the innovation priority and those who do not identify with it in the same ways. That is why we illustrated the significance of linking with the life of the congregation. When people are resistant to change, Adam Grant points out, "it helps to reinforce what will stay the same. Visions for change are more compelling when they include visions of continuity. Although our strategy might evolve, our identity will endure."[4]

Sustaining leadership and innovating leadership are not mutually exclusive. One is not better than the other. Each will have a priority depending on what chapter your congregation is facing on its journey. As a wise leader, you will always see that you are giving attention to both sustaining and innovating work so that your congregation can take its next faithful step.

Notes

INTRODUCTION. THE CHANGED CONTEXT FOR CHURCHES TODAY

1 Lovett H. Weems Jr., *Church Leadership: Vision, Team, Culture, and Integrity*, rev. ed. (Nashville: Abingdon, 2010), 1–3.

2 Max Weber, *The Sociology of Religion* (Boston: Beacon, 1993).

3 Ronald A. Heifetz and Marty Linsky, *Leadership on the Line: Staying Alive through the Dangers of Change* (Boston: Harvard Business School Press, 2002), 13–20.

4 Ronald A. Heifetz, *Leadership without Easy Answers* (Cambridge, MA: Harvard University Press, 1994), 22.

5 E. Brooks Holifield, *God's Ambassadors: A History of the Christian Clergy in America* (Grand Rapids, MI: Eerdmans, 2007), 7.

6 For a more extended discussion of the issues raised in the introduction as they apply specifically to mainline denominations, see Lovett H. Weems Jr., "Pastoral Leadership in Mainline Protestant Churches," in *Religious Leadership: A Reference Handbook*, ed. Sharon Henderson Callahan, 2 vols. (Thousand Oaks, CA: Sage, 2013), 91–98.

CHAPTER 1. SUSTAINING AND INNOVATING

1 Beverly Roberts Gaventa, *The Acts of the Apostles* (Nashville: Abingdon, 2003), 214.

2 Gaventa, 217.

3 Gaventa, 66.

4 Gaventa, 76.

5 Gaventa, 164.

CHAPTER 2. THE PASTORAL LEADERSHIP DILEMMA

1 For more on change as evolutionary more so than revolutionary, see Lovett H. Weems Jr., *Take the Next Step: Leading Lasting Change in the Church* (Nashville: Abingdon, 2003), 11–23.
2 James A. Harnish, *Extraordinary Ministry in Ordinary Time: An Invitation to Renewal for Pastors* (Nashville: Abingdon, 2019), 72.
3 Craig Dykstra, "Deep Veins of Wisdom," *Initiatives in Religion*, Lilly Endowment, Inc. (Summer 1993), 2.

CHAPTER 4. THE LEADER AS SUSTAINER

1 A book with resources for evaluating and improving your worship services is Lovett H. Weems Jr. and Tom Berlin, *Overflow: Increase Worship Attendance & Bear More Fruit* (Nashville: Abingdon, 2013).

CHAPTER 5. THE LEADER AS INNOVATOR

1 Peter F. Drucker, "The Theory of the Business," *Harvard Business Review* (September–October 1994), 95–96.

CHAPTER 6. SKILLS FOR SUSTAINING AND DISRUPTING

1 Lovett H. Weems Jr. and Tom Berlin, *Bearing Fruit: Ministry with Real Results* (Nashville: Abingdon, 2012), chap. 3.
2 Weems and Berlin, 21–23.

CHAPTER 7. TOOLS FOR DISCERNING YOUR NEXT FAITHFUL STEPS

1   Dorie Clark, "Feeling Stuck or Stymied?," *Harvard Business Review*, September–October 2021, 145.
2   Other tools are available, but this one is commonly used. Please note that you can locate most census data free of charge on the internet, so it is not necessary to pay for a census tool.

CHAPTER 8. A NEW MODEL FOR LEADING CHANGE

1   Heifetz and Linsky, *Leadership on the Line*, 13–20.
2   Matt Miofsky and Jason Byassee, *8 Virtues of Rapidly Growing Churches* (Nashville: Abingdon, 2018), 12.

CHAPTER 9. INNOVATING IN PRACTICE

1   Vijay Govindarajan and Chris Trimble, *The Other Side of Innovation: Solving the Execution Challenge* (Boston: Harvard Business School Press, 2010), 125.
2   Joan Magretta, *What Management Is: How It Works and Why It's Everybody's Business* (New York: Free Press, 2002), 65–70.
3   See the website of Lewis Center for Church Leadership of Wesley Theological Seminary, https://www.churchleadership.com.
4   Adam Grant, *Think Again: The Power of Knowing What You Don't Know* (New York: Viking, 2021), 31.

Recommended Resources

Anthony, Scott D., Clark G. Gilbert, and Mark W. Johnson. *Dual Transformation: How to Reposition Today's Business While Creating the Future*. Boston: Harvard Business Review Press, 2017.

The authors worked with Clayton Christensen. They understand sustaining and disruptive innovation well. In this book, they describe the process of strengthening Transformation A (the current core) and developing Transformation B (the future that's needed).

Baughman, Michael, ed. *Flipping Church: How Successful Church Planters Are Turning Conventional Wisdom Upside-Down*. Nashville: Upper Room Books, 2016.

This anthology shares innovative practices from successful church planters that help all pastors imagine a new way forward. Readers will benefit from leaders with a wide range of views from diverse settings who will aid them in their own contextual practices.

Beaumont, Susan. *How to Lead When You Don't Know Where You're Going: Leading in a Liminal Season*. Lanham, MD: Rowman & Littlefield, 2019.

Beaumont writes for an in-between time in which none of us feel prepared. She draws upon authenticity, discernment, memory, and purpose to give hope and direction to congregational leaders and uses marvelous examples.

Govindarajan, Vijay, and Chris Trimble. *The Other Side of Innovation: Solving the Execution Challenge*. Boston: Harvard Business Review Press, 2010.

The authors describe the tension between managing current operations while simultaneously leading innovation. While they write in the business world, many of their principles and practices hold true for all organizations.

Powe, F. Douglas, Jr. *The Adept Church: Navigating between a Rock and a Hard Place*. Nashville: Abingdon, 2020.

Powe offers a methodical, logical approach for strategic development and decision-making. This book offers a clear process for showing congregations how to define their reality and a map showing the way to move forward.

Rendle, Gil. *Quietly Courageous: Leading the Church in a Changing Time*. Lanham, MD: Rowman & Littlefield, 2018.

Rendle understands how difficult it is for churches to move beyond mere incremental change, which is utterly insufficient for the challenges of our time. Innovative leadership faces far more challenges than the use of time and energy. Rendle explores how the assumptions on which the church operates now are so powerful that they act to constrain innovation. The church tends to redefine innovation to fit currently accepted assumptions and practices that no longer apply.

Zscheile, Dwight J. *The Agile Church: Spirit-Led Innovation in an Uncertain Age*. New York: Morehouse, 2014.

Zscheile writes for traditional churches immobilized in the face of a radically changed culture. He understands that innovation must be a way of life for churches in the next decades. Churches practicing his "traditioned innovation," in which they make "good mistakes," learn from them, and move on quickly, have a chance to bear vital witness.